Daily Lifelines

for Teens & Preteens

Testimonials

"Filled with wise solutions to teenage problems, this book teaches character-building and self awareness."
Sean Covey
The 7 Habits of Highly Effective Teens

"This book is beautiful in its soul soothing message and profound in its simplicity. Although it is directed to teens, adults will find it comforting and useful."
Annie Kirkwood
Messages to the Family

"As a minister I'm always looking for ways to reach our youth and this guide is an excellent tool. Using the scriptures to affirm the realities of life is a masterful stroke in character building, self-appraisal and building a lasting relationship not only with one another but also with God.
The Bible asks a searching question: "How can you say that you love God whom you have never seen and hate your brother who you see every day?"
Rev. Robert L. Barney Sr.

"This book is perfect for preteens and teens. Also, for parents of teenagers. The prayers are short, unique and inspiring. It is a daily 'shot in the arm' to remind kids to turn to God in their daily lives."
        Sister John Mandeville, C.S.U.

"It helped me in my spiritual life. It made me care more about being open to others."
               Brandi Ball, 12

"I enjoyed the writing activities and felt children would gain insight into their inner selves by doing them."
             Julie S. Knocke
                Youth Leader

"There is a real need for this type of a directed journal for middle school kids. I really appreciate the variety of topics. It seems as if every topic imaginable is confronted at some point in the 365 days.

I grew to crave the action statement. It spelled out for the youth what they needed to do to get results."
              Jennifer Cox
              Youth Leader

"Great for parents. It puts you back in the mind of your children and how they think. What better way is there to help them through a situation than to feel and think what they are thinking and feeling."
           Mary Beth Mueller
          Parent of two teen sons

Daily Lifelines
for Teens & Preteens

Teaches Values and Common Sense Tools
for Leading Confident Lives

by Diane M. Keefe

Lifelines Publishing Company
P. O. Box 700
Eureka, MO 63025

Lifelines Publishing Company
P. O. Box 700
Eureka, MO 63025
Copyright © 2001 by Diane M. Keefe

Cover designer: Robert Howard
Illustrator: Phil Benson
Editor: Carolyn Kruse

All rights reserved, including the right to reproduce this book or portions thereof in any form whatsoever. For reproduction permission write Diane Keefe, Lifelines Publishing Company, P.O. Box 700, Eureka, MO 63025.

Library of Congress Control Number: 2001126427

Keefe, Diane M.
    Daily lifelines for teens and preteens : teaches values and common sense tools for leading confident lives / by Diane M. Keefe. -- 1st ed.
    p. cm.
    Includes bibliographical references and index.
    Audience: Ages 9-15.
    ISBN 0-9710447-0-8

    1. Teenagers--Conduct of life--Juvenile literature.
2. Teenagers--Life skills guides--Juvenile literature.
3. Self-realization--Juvenile literature. 4. Teenagers --Spiritual life--Juvenile literature. [1. Conduct of life. 2. Life skills.] I. Title

BJ1661.D35 2002   158.1′28′0835
                              QBI01-700529

*This book is dedicated to my daughters,
Robyn and Shannon*

ACKNOWLEDGMENTS

I would like to thank my husband, who gave encouragement, suggestions, and support; Jan Kelo (retired 5th and 6th grade teacher) and Maria Sulecki (Youth Leader at Unity and Spiritual Friend), who read the lessons and gave critical feedback. I especially thank Dr. Carolyn Kruse for her support and encouragement; Scottie Priesmeyer, self publishing mentor; Beth Hayes, copyeditor; Phil Benson, illustrator; Joan Herron, page layout; and Dr. Roxanne Delcau, friend. Gratitude is in order to Annie Kirkwood, author of *Messages to the Family, Messages of Hope,* and *Mary's Message to the World,* for her encouragement and insights into the business of publishing. Thanks go to Sean Covey, *The 7 Habits of Highly Effective Teens,* for his review, as well as those of Julie Knocke, Rev. Robert Barney, Sr., Sister John Mandeville, Jennifer Cox, Brandi Ball, and Mary Beth Mueller.

Thanks also for the copyright permissions from Dr. William Tiller, Nebraska Press, The Center for Non-Violent Communication, Walter Weston, Joel Arthur Barker, and Blue Dolphin Publishing, Inc.

Others who supported me and/or reviewed parts of the book and provided feedback include: Priscilla Norling (Spiritual Life Director at The Federated Church in Chagrin Falls, Ohio); Mark Simone (Youth Minister at Federated Church); Kathy Simone (Art Teacher); Darlene Hall (Pediatrician); Dr. Walter Weston (Minister and Healer); Audrey McDonald (Spiritual Facilitator); Kate Wenger (Student); Chris McInnis (Person Extraordinaire); Debra Glowik (YMCA); Lou Frebourne (Breath Work Facilitator); Allison (Best Friend and Mother); Jessica and Charlotte Bigelow (Students); Janice and Mike Malovasic (Friends and Neighbors); and Ilona Chambre; Joan Kendig and her mother, Rose; and Terry McFaul (Spiritual Friends). To any others who supported me from afar, thank you for your encouragement. Without it I am not sure I would have been able to reach completion.

I especially thank God for facilitating this journey, inspiring me in the lessons, and placing such wonderful, capable people in my path.

Thank You, God!

PREFACE

Dear Parents,

Daily Lifelines will provide you with the tools to teach your teens about values and techniques that will help them be successful in life. This book provides an opportunity for discussing key issues of concern to teens a calm manner and while everyone is receptive. *Daily Lifelines* was written as a perpetual calendar, meaning that it can be used over again, and that the reader can begin at any time of the year. The Index allows readers to skip ahead to pertinent topics or review back as many times as they wish.

I wrote this book because I needed a way to introduce my children to core values and all of the spiritual healing information I had been learning. It seemed that when I thought about discussing these things with them, it was when they had done something I did not like and I was disciplining them. That was not the right time to teach them. The inspiration for the book came to me one night during meditation. Once the ideas began to flow, I could hardly turn them off.

It is my hope that this daily meditation guide will provide a vehicle for other parents to teach their children these concepts under more receptive conditions. If there is a topic with which you have a problem, use the opportunity to make your position known.

Choose a time when everyone is calm, such as before bedtime, first thing in the morning, in the car while waiting for someone, and so on. Select the best time, when the child can think about the lesson and put the thought into practice that day.

My own children were 8 and 10 when I began to write this. They have been fully capable of reading and understanding the lessons and asking questions. You may wish to read with younger children so they can ask questions as you read together. Some concepts may be too complex for some children to understand right now, but they may pick it up next year. The readings plant the seed. Never underestimate children. The nice thing about meditation guides is that they may be read over and over again. I have found that certain topics pop up just when I am ready to deal with them!

Each daily meditation contains a topical lesson, an affirmation, or a positive statement about what the child will do, and a prayer. Every lesson is interactive in that the child is encouraged to respond to the lesson topic in actions or words.

I wrestled with what to call God. Some people call God Yahweh, Abba, Higher Power, Divine Intelligence, Creator, Mother-Father God, and so on. In writing these lessons, I purposely tried not to assign gender to God. In some cases I used "he" and in other "she." I believe that we can all agree that God is more than we can imagine, and therefore trying to define God is fruitless. I used "God" and will leave it up to you to call God what you wish. I do not think that God cares.

Many people are experiencing a spiritual renewal and want to share this with their children. I hope this book will help you and your children.

To Young Readers,

A walk with God is an inner journey, not an outer journey. The purpose is to uncover the fears and illusions you hold that keep God from expressing through you. As you rid yourself of fears and incorrect thinking, you are free to experience God's love, peace, and joy in your life. This is your goal—to heal yourself and to become aware of God's presence in your life. Your communication with God must become part of your daily habit and routine.

How to Use this Book: This book can be used anytime during the day when you feel quiet and reflective. Feel free to skip ahead to lessons that feel right for the present time. Draw pictures or color in the illustrations if you feel so moved. The Index makes it easy to choose topics of interest if you wish to skip ahead or just review. You can go back as many times as you wish.

Each page contains a lesson. Here is a lesson on meditating:

HOW TO MEDITATE

The way you choose to meditate is individual. There is no one way to meditate as long as the method you choose works for you. The object of meditation is to quiet your mind and be receptive to God's ideas and input. Therefore meditating to rock music might not be a good choice.

1. **Choose a quiet spot.** ...maybe in your favorite tree or in a favorite chair. You may wish to listen to quiet music in the background or maybe not.

2. **Begin with the intention of connecting to God.** Imagine yourself surrounded by God's light. If you wish to meditate on a specific topic, state it now. Or you might ask your inner guide for a topic that is for your highest good.

3. **Choose a consistent time.** Maybe before bed or first thing in the morning would be the best time. When you develop consistency in meditation, you will find your whole body begins to get ready for the meditation. In the beginning, you may only be able to do 5 to 10 minutes. As you progress, you will be guided in your growth.

4. **Relax.** Take a nice, deep breath. Hold it for 3 seconds, and then let it out slowly. Do this 20 times. Note your feet relaxing, and then proceed through each body part until everything is relaxed.

You may wish to chant the word-intention of your meditation, for example, "peace" or "love." If a stray thought comes in, acknowledge it and let it go. Ask to be connected with others praying or meditating on the same intention. When you finish, give thanks.

Next, you will see an affirmation. An affirmation is a positive action statement about how you want to live your life. Here is an example:

Today I will begin meditating for at least 5 to 10 minutes. I will quiet my chatter and listen to God.

Then you will see a prayer supporting the lesson. This is a sample prayer. You will be asked to participate in the lesson, so have a pen and paper ready. You may wish to purchase a notebook or writing journal to record your thoughts.

Dear God,

I am ready to listen to you. Guide me in finding the time and way to meditate that are right for me. Help me to know when I am on the right track.

Thank you, God!

Last, you will find an action item.

This is a sample action item:

> Practice meditating for 5 to 10 minutes now. If I cannot do it now, I will meditate later at _____ (time).

I hope this book will help you to grow in wisdom and maturity and, most importantly, to grow spiritually. May you find your connection to your Creator growing stronger each day, and may your life become more loving and joyful.

With love,

Diane Keefe

PHOTOS
(New friends and family)

January 1
NEW YEAR'S GOALS

The first day of the New Year presents an excellent time to set new goals. After reflecting on what you did in the past year and on what you learned, think about which goals you would like to continue from the previous year and new goals that you would like to add.

For example, you may have set a goal to develop as a soccer player or to keep high grades in school. You may decide to carry over those goals into the New Year as well. If there is a new technique you would like to learn in soccer or perhaps study skills you would like to improve, list these goals. Are there other goals you would like to add?

Look at your goals. Limit yourself to no more than 3 or 4 items. Otherwise you might not be able to keep up with them. Post them in a place where you can refer to them often to check your progress.

Today I will write down my goals for the New Year and post them where I can see how I am doing.

Dear God,

Help me in setting attainable goals. I ask your help in reaching them by the end of this year.

Thank you, God!

My goals:
1. do well in school
2. do well in dance
3. don't get into sports
4. Grow a stronger spiritual relationship

January 2
DIVINE ORDER

When you go to school, you know what to expect when you get there. Everything has been put in order so you will have teachers, gym, library time, transportation, and so on. You can trust what happens there. The opposite of order is chaos. Chaos means that you cannot know what to expect. War is an example of chaos. Chaos is destructive, or it may provide the illusion of being destructive while breaking down the old order. Then a new order is established.

God has a Divine Plan for each of us. God has placed our universe in Divine Order. We know that the sun will rise and set and that we will have a change of seasons. We know that we arrive through birth, live our lifetime, and then die a physical death. All is in Divine Order.

If you feel that your life and the way you have chosen to live it are in chaos, ask God to bring Divine Order back into your life. Surrender your will to God and watch miracles occur!

Today I will go with the flow. I will be flexible in chaos and appreciative of the order around me.

Dear God,

Thank you for the order in my life. Where there is chaos, give me guidance to make it through, trusting in your Divine Plan. Let me not be the cause of my own unnecessary chaos.

Thank you, God!

I can clear chaos today by:
Not runnin my big mouth

January 3
LOVE ONE ANOTHER AS I HAVE LOVED YOU

Jesus taught us to love one another. Sometimes that is difficult when we get into an argument and cannot come to a compromise. We can choose to respect the other person even if we can't agree. We are all made in the likeness of God. Try to understand the other person's point of view. The Native Americans have a saying "Do not judge another until you have walked a mile in his moccasins."

Loving another can also mean caring and showing compassion if that person is homeless and needs help with food and basic needs.

Today I will love myself and others by showing compassion and care.

Dear God,

Teach me to love as you have loved. Help me to overlook differing points of view and to view the other person as one of your creation. Help the smile on my face to put a smile on another's face. I will be your loving child today.

Thank you, God!

One way I can do this today is:

_____
_____
_____
_____

January 4
BEING AT PEACE

Being at peace is experiencing a calm state of mind. When walking outside, witness the beauty of God's creation...the trees, birds, fresh smell of the wind, colors of the sky. Take a walk in the woods and feel the presence of God in it.

If I am not feeling at peace, I can ask for God's help to get back that feeling of peace. Then I can do something to bring it about...a nice, warm bath; listening to beautiful music; inviting a friend over; playing with a pet; or taking a walk.

Today I will participate in activities that will bring about peace in my life. I will model a peaceful nature to others.

Dear God,

Today I want to feel your peace. Surround me in your peaceful energy and help me to choose activities that will contribute to my being at peace.

Thank you, God!

Three things I can do today to bring about peace in my life are:
1. _____
2. _____
3. _____

January 5
JOY

Joy is an intense feeling of happiness. We can experience God's gift of joy through walks in nature, contact with a friend, a trip to the amusement park, or anything that makes us happy. Amazingly, when we give of ourselves to others, we feel intense joy. It is important to thank God for these gifts of joy—whether simple or more elaborate.

Today I will take note of those things that bring me joy and give thanks to God! I will write them in my journal.

Dear God,

Thank you for the joy in my life. When I am feeling down, remind me of those things that bring me joy.

Thank you, God!

Things that bring me joy:
- talkin to certain people
- goin out with friends
- listenin to good music

January 6

UNSELFISHNESS

When I am being unselfish, it means that I am thinking about someone else's needs as well as my own. When I am being unselfish, I am able to share. God's love is reflecting through me. I am being unselfish when I pick up after myself, when I offer someone else the first choice on an item we are sharing, and when I offer my jacket to someone who is cold.

Today I will monitor my behavior and be aware of other's needs as well as my own.

Dear God,

I know you love me beyond measure. You take care of the birds of the air and the animals of the forest. You provide for all my needs, so Lord, please help me to care for others as you care for me.

Thank you, God!

Ways I can be unselfish: thinking of others

January 7
GIVING OF ONESELF

How many ways can I give of myself? God created each person on earth to have unique gifts and talents. Each person is different. Because we are different from one another, we can offer to each other the gifts or talents God has given to us. The gift you share might be a unique outlook on some topic...it might be a listening ear...or it might be a special skill. To share your gifts, you must believe they have value.

Also, sharing your gifts with others will give you intense joy and feelings of self-worth.

Today I will take note of my unique gifts and share them with others.

Dear God,

Help me to realize my own talents and share them with others. Help me, too, to appreciate the gifts or talents others share with me.

Thank you, God!

Some of the gifts and talents God has given to me are:

_____
_____
_____
_____
_____
_____

January 8
MAKING CHOICES

We are in charge of our lives. God has given every person or child on earth the freedom to make choices regarding his or her life. The choices that we make determine the quality of our life. Many times we act on impulse without thinking of what the consequences might be. Then we are sorry.

Think of a decision you made today or yesterday. How did you handle it? What were your alternatives? What were the consequences?

_____
_____
_____
_____
_____

Today, God, I will try to think of the consequences of my choices before I act, knowing that you are always available and willing to help if I ask you.

Dear God,

I ask your help and guidance in making choices in my life. Help me to make choices that are good for me and honor others as well.

Thank you, God!

January 9
CELEBRATING YOURSELF

We are all creations of God. We were made in the image of God, and we can celebrate the uniqueness that is ours.

Today I will take note of everything that helps me be aware that I am growing and constantly changing. I will write it down so that I can read it again when I forget how special I am.

Dear God,

Thank you for my life. When I am being hard on myself for any reason, remind me to read again the description I have written of how I am special. Remind me that you do not create junk. Help me celebrate the special blessing of being a child of God.

Thank you, God!

Ways I am growing and changing and ways that I am special:

New thoughts
New experiences
I'm my own self

January 10
BEING ON THE PATH

We are all on a spiritual journey throughout our lives. Every time we encounter a problem or difficulty, we are given the opportunity to solve it. Through prayer and keeping a close relationship with God, we can learn our lessons faster. When we look back, we are able to see what we learned. Keeping a journal or diary can help you to see your growth more clearly and to work through your problems. Answers to problems become more clear when you are able to organize your thoughts by writing them down or talking about them with a friend or trusted adult.

Today I will look at each problem or difficulty in my life as an opportunity to grow.

Dear God,

I ask your guidance in tackling the difficult times in my life. Remind me to ask for your help so I will be able to grow in your Wisdom and Understanding.

Thank you, God!

Problems I am facing:
Self Esteem,
Decisions & Choices

January 11
LETTING GO OF ANGER

When you are angry, it shuts off your creative energy and ability to love. Anger that is not let go may turn into an illness in the body. Anger is usually caused by a fear...perhaps you feel threatened somehow. Ask yourself, "What is the fear behind this anger?" Then ask God to help you release the anger from your system. You can do this through prayer.

> Place your hand over your heart. Ask God to release your anger through your hand to God's loving care. Then ask God to bring in Divine Love, Peace, and Joy to replace the anger. Give thanks.[1]

Today I choose to release any negative feelings or emotions from my body. I will forgive anyone who has ever hurt me.

Dear God,

I ask you to help me release this anger into your loving care. Please replace it with your Joy and Peace.

Thank you, God!

January 12

*Today
I feel the
love of God
surrounding all of me.
I can never
be separated from
the love of God.*

Thank you, God!

January 13
LETTING GO OF JEALOUSY

Jealousy is envy carried one step further. A person who is jealous may say things behind another person's back or tell lies in order to hurt someone. A jealous person actually hurts himself or herself worse than the other person. Jealousy will make you feel less of a person than you really are.

Today I will watch my thoughts and actions. If I find myself being jealous, I will ask God to help me release it. Perhaps I can even be a friend to the other person. When I realize my own true worth, I will be able to see the value of others.

Dear God,

When I find myself being jealous, help me to see my own true worth. Help me to be a friend to everyone.

Thank you, God!

I am feeling jealous about:
Nothing I envy but not jealous

January 14
GOSSIPING

Gossiping happens when you talk about others when they are not present. Gossip is often hearsay, which means someone who was not directly involved reported it—it may or may not be true. Gossip can hurt others. It is unkind. If you do not want someone to talk about you, you should not talk about anyone else.

We are all growing, and we all will have actions that we wish could be different. Instead of pointing out others' faults or misbehaviors, realize that others are growing just as you are. Ask what you can learn from another person's failure. What could that person learn from yours?

Today I will not participate in gossip, which might hurt others. Instead, I will look for what I can learn from my own mistakes and from those of others.

Dear God,

Help me to be aware when I am being pulled into gossip. Help me to always show respect to myself and to others. Also help me to see what there is to learn from my mistakes and those of others.

Thank you, God!

Ways I can learn from my mistakes:
_____
_____
_____
_____
_____

January 15

TRUSTING IN YOUR HIGHER POWER

Sometimes when we've had a bad day and our spirits are low, we do not feel God's presence.

God is always with us and willing to help if we will only ask. Ask for God's help to face your difficulties. Perhaps you need help with a friend. Then you can ask God to make your friendship happy and at peace again.

Today I will be aware of God's presence and ask for Divine guidance.

Dear God,

Help me to remember that you are always there ready to help me when I ask. Now I ask your help with _____
_____
_____
_____

I put this in your loving care.

Thank you, God!

January 16

FORGIVENESS OF ONESELF AND OTHERS

Forgiveness means letting go of a hurt or injury. Sometimes when a friend makes fun of us or hurts us in some way, we cut off our love to that person. Jesus taught that forgiveness was important to our growth. When we refuse to forgive another or ourselves, we become stuck and cannot move on because we are turning away from God.

Sometimes it is hard to forgive. We may need to pray for this over time. Do not be discouraged if you are unable to forgive right away. Keep asking for God's help.

Today I will ask God for help in forgiving

Dear God,

Sometimes I do something for which I am ashamed or embarrassed and I feel I cannot forgive myself. I put this in your loving care, and I ask you to help me let go of it. Sometimes I cannot forgive a friend or family member for their behavior toward me. Help me to let go of it. Surround us all in the light of your love. Help us mend our hearts.

Thank you, God!

January 17

LETTING YOUR LIGHT SHINE

When someone says to let your light shine bright, the person is referring to the love of God. God's love shines through us when we show a kindness to others or when we treat others with respect.

Today I will let my light shine by being the best that I can be and by treating everyone I meet as my friend. I know I am Divinely Protected and Loved.

Dear God,

Allow your light to shine brightly through me. Surround everyone I meet today in your love.

Thank you, God!

Ways I will shine my light today:
_____
_____
_____
_____

January 18

HONORING YOURSELF AND OTHERS

Jesus said, "Love one another as I have loved you."

Honoring is a word that means showing great respect or holding in high regard. When I give honor to myself or others, I show God that I appreciate the gift of life he gave to me and that I will try to be the best person I can be in my thought and behavior toward myself and others.

Today I will honor myself by taking good care of my body and by being patient with myself during my daily trials. I will honor others by treating them with respect and courtesy. I will honor God's earth by taking care of it and not using more than I need.

Dear God,

Help me to be an example of "honoring" to myself and others. Help me to model Jesus in treating others with love and compassion.

Thank you, God!

Ways I am honoring myself and others today:

_____
_____
_____
_____
_____

January 19

MAKING FUN OF OTHERS OR CALLING NAMES

Sometimes when we are spending time with friends, an argument begins that results in calling the other person names or making fun of the person. Sometimes, even without an argument being involved, we make fun of others and it hurts their feelings. When this happens, we must ask ourselves, "Is this the way we wish to be treated?" Jesus said, "Love one another as I have loved you." This means treating each other with love and respect. It also means asking for forgiveness if we were the one who started it...or forgiving others if they do it to you.

Today I will treat others with love and respect. I will not call anyone a name or make fun of anyone.

Dear God,

Please teach me to love my neighbors as myself and to be a good model for others.

Thank you, God!

Ways I can show love and respect to others today:
_____
_____
_____
_____

January 20

*Today I am on
the path
back to God.
God's light shows
me the way.*

Thank you, God!

January 21

HONORING PEOPLE OF ALL COLORS

God created us all, and God's spark reflects through all of us. God is so immense that there are many ways in which God's being is expressed. When creating people, God created many sizes and shapes and colors. Although people look different on the outside, we are all the same inside. We all have a spirit, a body, emotions, likes and dislikes, and needs for food and shelter.

In the past, people of different colors separated themselves from each other by pretending to be better than other races. God would not want this. Rather, it is best to honor each other because the presence of God resides in all of us. By seeing how much we are alike, we realize that we are all part of the family of God.

One way you can understand more about this is by getting to know people of other races. Hosting an exchange student is a good way to learn about other cultures and races. Travel or become involved in activities that promote multicultural and racial awareness.

Today I will take a new look at people of different colors. I will look for how we are the same. I will seek to understand rather than to be understood.

Dear God,

Help me to understand my place in the family of God. Teach me more about other cultures and races. Develop in me an open heart and mind.

Thank you, God!

Ways people from all races and cultures are alike:
_____
_____

January 22
PICKING FIGHTS

Sometimes it seems just part of the daily communication of young people to fight. A young person may be entertaining himself or herself quietly and a sibling comes in and takes a CD or does something to annoy the other...destroying the peace and joy.

We might ask, "What is my part in this? What is the other person needing?" Perhaps they want a friend and just do not know how to ask.

Today, if I get into a fight with a friend or sibling, I will try to observe what my part is and how I am feeling. I will ask myself what the other person might be feeling or needing. What does God ask us to do here? Do we need to forgive each other?

Dear God,

When I get involved in fights, help me to understand what is happening and how peace can be regained again. Also help us to grow from it and forgive each other.

Thank you, God!

Reflect on a time when you were involved in a fight. What did you want? What did the other person truly need?

_____
_____
_____
_____
_____

January 23
BRINGING JOY TO OTHERS

Each child of God was created with a unique beauty within. Young people can share their enthusiasm, ready smiles, humor, and helpfulness. Those are easy gifts to share with others. What other gifts can you think of that you can share with others? Gifts do not have to cost money, and often the best ones are free—like hugs, gifts of your time, or giving attention to others. The surprise is in what you receive back—joy, peace, and feeling good about yourself.

Today I will think of things I can do that will allow me to share of myself with others.

Dear God,

Help me to share of my gifts with others. And help me to be able to receive other's gifts too.

Thank you, God!

How can I bring joy to others today?

_____
_____
_____
_____
_____

January 24
BUILDING TRUST

Trust means that you believe that God loves you and will care for you even in the most difficult situations. We must trust that God has a greater good planned for us when things are not going the way we hoped they would.

God is only good and loves us so much. It is God's pleasure to give us those things that will be good for us. God cares for the birds of the air and the animals of the earth. They do not worry about where they will find their next meal or shelter over their heads. We must trust God in the same way.

Today when I want something, I will tell God what it is and then trust that what I've asked for or something better will come.

Dear God,
I want to trust you just as the animals of your kingdom do. Help me to know that you will always bring me what is in my highest good.

Thank you, God!

Ways that I am trusting God today:

_____
_____
_____
_____
_____

January 25
BEING DISCERNING

When you are able to be discerning, it means that you will be able to tell the difference between whether something is truth or not. Information and ideas come to us daily and even hourly. Our friends may try to influence us to do something about which we don't feel right. We may feel uneasy. That feeling is our inner voice—placed there by God—telling us that this is not the right thing to do. Always trust your inner voice! If you are not sure what to do, tell your friend you need time to think about it. Then pray to God to be clear about what you should do. Be mindful of consequences.

Today I will let my inner voice tell me if something is truth or not. I will listen to my inner voice to help guide me, and I will ask God what I should do.

Dear God,

Sometimes I don't know what to do. Help me to do the right thing. Help me to trust my own inner guidance.

Thank you, God!

Times today when I will tune in to my inner voice:
_____
_____
_____
_____
_____
_____

January 26
TELLING SECRETS

When a friend has a secret and won't tell you, it might make you feel left out and unimportant or it might make you feel like your friend is saying something about you that he or she doesn't want you to hear. This is how someone else might feel if you have a secret that you won't tell.

Only in sharing do we realize that we are all the same. We have the same needs, problems, and situations in our lives. When we share, we make friends.

However, some secrets don't need to be shared with everyone. Respect other's privacy and feelings.

Today I will avoid secrets. Instead, I will share things that will make others feel good about themselves. This will open a path to new friendships and sharing.

Dear God,

Steer me away from secrets toward a path of sharing with others. Bless me with many friends.

Thank you, God!

Things I will share today:

_____
_____
_____
_____
_____
_____

January 27

*Today
I feel the Peace
of God
growing
ever more deeply
within me.*

Thank you, God!

January 28

RESPECTING SOMEONE ELSE'S PROPERTY

You can show respect for someone else's property by keeping it in good condition, treating it with respect. Return it in the condition in which you received it, or if it becomes damaged while you use it, repair it or replace it before returning it. By showing respect for someone else's property, you are showing respect for the person who owns it.

Today I will treat others' property with respect. I will handle it as if it were my own or even better. This will honor the person who owns it.

Dear God,

Sometimes when I use someone else's property, it becomes broken or damaged. Help me to forgive myself and get the damaged item repaired or replace it. Please don't allow 'things' to come between my friends and me. God, I ask you to help me to do the right thing always.

Thank you, God!

Ways I can respect others' property today:

_____
_____
_____
_____
_____

January 29

WHAT A DIFFERENCE ONE PERSON CAN MAKE

When Princess Diana died, the entire world grieved. She was noted for her compassion for her fellow humans and her good works. She was a model humanitarian for the world. Her life was like a rock being thrown in a pond. It made big ripples. Mother Teresa was also such a person. She worked selflessly to help the poor of India.

What kind of ripple would your life make if you were no longer on earth? What would people remember about you? On a piece of paper, write your own obituary. For what would you like to be remembered? Now make plans to make it so.

Today I will begin to make plans to make my ripples on the world. When I die, I want to be remembered for:

_____
_____
_____

Dear God,

Guide my efforts to make a difference. Help me work to my highest good and potential.

Thank you, God!

January 30
BEING STILL TO HEAR GOD'S VOICE

When you are praying, you are talking to God. When you meditate or allow yourself to be quiet, you give God an opportunity to talk to you.

Often your most creative thoughts or solutions to problems will come when you are in quiet reflection. In today's world, we wake up to noise—alarm clocks, radios, TVs, computers, the sound of cars and buses. That's why it is important for you to set aside time every day for quiet reflection. You will have to find the best time for you. Some people are able to meditate while walking in nature or doing hard physical exercise.

If you do it the same time every day, you will be more successful in remembering to do it. Also, remember that when God talks to you, it will not be in a loud voice. You may not hear anything, but you will find that just at time that you need it, the right thought will jump into your brain or you will just know what you are to do.

Today I will make time to spend in quiet reflection with God.

Dear God,

Help me to be disciplined in talking to you as well as listening to you. I know you are there to guide me, if only I will listen or ask for help.

Thank you, God!

The best time for me to meditate is:

_____

January 31
EATING THE RIGHT FOODS

It is your responsibility to learn about proper nutrition and feed your body the right kind of foods. As you become more in tune with your body, it will tell you which ones are good for it and which are not. It is also important to get the right amount of rest and exercise.

Today I will appreciate my body for the great gift it is. I will take steps to learn about the right foods to eat to keep my body well tuned and healthy.

Dear God,

I am grateful for the body you have given me. Help me to get in tune with its needs and to be a good caretaker.

Thank you, God!

Ways I will care for my body respectfully today:
_____
_____
_____
_____
_____

February 1
DEALING WITH DEATH

Dying is a natural part of life. It is part of the cycle of life. When a person dies, his or her soul continues to live on. The person's soul goes to be with God.

Young people and adults feel sad, afraid, and even angry when a loved one leaves them. They are sad because they will not see that person again until they die and reach heaven. They are afraid because sometimes their circumstances of living may change as a result of the person's death. They may even feel angry at the person for dying or at God for letting the person die. This is normal. That person will always be part of your memories. You can talk to the person in your mind.

Talk to God or write in your journal about your feelings. In time, the intensity of your feelings will lessen. Ask God for comfort and to help you come to a feeling of peace about it. Treasure the times you spent with the person who died. Make a photo album or scrapbook about the times you spent together.

Today I will comfort anyone who loses someone close to them. I will just be there for them. I do not need to say anything other than "I am sorry for your loss."

Dear God,

Losing someone close is tough. Help me to give myself some time to grieve and process my feelings. Help me to be there for others by offering my friendship and presence.

Thank you, God!

My feelings about death:

_____

_____

February 2
BEING AT PEACE IN NATURE

When I lie down in the middle of a yard or field, I can smell the grass and flowers. I can feel the wind caressing my body and see the beautiful blue sky and puffy clouds. The sun feels warm and comforting. A nearby tree shields me from too much sun. I feel at peace. God is taking care of me.

When I am in times of trouble, I can remember what it is like to be in that peace. God comforts me.

Today I will experience God's peace and comfort. I will spend some time in God's nature being alone with God and experiencing peace.

Dear God,

Sometimes I am so busy that I do not take the time to see the beauty of the world around me or to feel its peace. Help me to remember that you offer me your peace when I ask for it. Help me to always be in your peace.

Thank you, God!

Best time today to "stop" and see the beauty of the world:

_____
_____
_____
_____

February 3
BE WITH A FRIEND

Being with friends can bring great joy and also provide opportunities for our growth and support. When a friend is being sad about something, we can be there for him or her with a listening ear and compassionate heart. By listening and sharing our experiences, we teach each other about life. We can be joy filled when something good happens to our friends. We help them celebrate.

Friends are one of the greatest gifts God gives us. Friends will listen when we need to talk. As friends, we share our innermost thoughts.

Today I will do something nice to let my friend know I appreciate him or her.

Dear God,

Thank you for my friends. My friends and I share good times and bad times. We enjoy each other and comfort one another. This is one of the ways you bring good into my life. Thank you for being my friend.

Thank you, God!

What I will do to be a good friend:
_____
_____
_____
_____

February 4
TAKING TIME OUT FOR MYSELF

Perhaps I am doing homework or participating in sports, playing with my brothers and sisters, or running to lessons. Whew! Next thing I know it's time for bed. Where did my day go?

Today I will take time just for myself to do what I like to do and treat myself well. I will reward myself for studying hard or practicing hard by doing something I find relaxing. I will take time to appreciate myself, a gift from God.

Dear God,

Thank you for the gift of myself. Help me remember to take time to appreciate myself and reward myself when I work hard.

Thank you, God!

What I am doing today to appreciate myself:
_____
_____
_____
_____
_____

February 5
WHEN THINGS SEEM OVERWHELMING

Sometimes when we are given a project to do by our teachers or a parent asks us to clean up our room, we may feel we can never get it done. We may feel overwhelmed.

It helps to break it down into little steps. In the case of a project, agree to do only 1 or 2 steps per day. Pretty soon the project is done and you say, "That wasn't so bad! I can do it!" However, if you wait until the last minute, you feel panicked, anxious, and very stressed.

Today I approach each project I encounter by breaking it down into small, workable steps. Then I will not be overwhelmed by the size of the task.

Dear God,

I can do anything as long as I can break it down into small, workable steps. Help me to face any large task by asking for your guidance. With you as my partner, I cannot fail!

Thank you, God!

These are the small, workable steps of a problem I am now completing:
1. _____
2. _____
3. _____
4. _____
5. _____

February 6
I FEEL LIKE I DISAPPOINTED SOMEONE TODAY

Perhaps I did not do my best today. I feel like I disappointed someone. It makes me feel sad and not very good about myself.

I am happy when I feel your love around me, God. I know I will do better next time. I know you love me no matter what I do. I need not feel bad about myself but instead will look for the lesson I need to learn in this situation.

Today I will remember that I can always count on God's love. Mistakes and bad days are there to help us reflect on how we can do better and learn from what we did.
Today I will learn from my mistakes and do a better job next time. I will forgive myself for whatever I did.

Dear God,

Thank you for loving us through good times and bad. Help me to see the gift of learning you have brought to me.

Thank you, God!

I forgive myself for: _____

What I learned is: _____

February 7
ROLE MODELS

Role models are the people you admire and want to imitate as you grow up. They can be famous people, like sports figures and actresses, or the people you know, like aunts and uncles, grandparents, or teachers and coaches. It is important to read about people of history to find out about their successes and failures. How did they handle them? What goals did they set for themselves?

If you have an idea of what you would like to do when you grow up, find people who have already done it. Ask them how they got started. What successes and failures have they had?

_____
_____
_____

How did they handle them? _____
_____
_____
_____

Today I will look for positive role models in my life— perhaps someone in a career I think I might like or maybe just someone I admire and want to be like. I will ask questions about the person's life and the choices he or she made.

Dear God,

Help me gain insight on how people have handled the successes and failures in their lives. Surround me with good role models.

Thank you, God!

February 8

*Today
God's love pours down
on me.
I am forgiven of
everything.
Each day is a
new beginning.*

Thank you, God!

February 9
ACCEPTING OTHERS

Danny is different. He goes to the beat of his own drum. Alicia is quiet and shy; she never says very much. Sara has carrot-colored hair and bubbles over with enthusiasm. Sometimes they argue over topics introduced by their teacher, or sometimes they argue over the games they play. They know they can respect each other without having to agree with each other's ideas or behavior. It's OK to have your own ideas.

Sometimes by listening to everyone's ideas, the very best ideas can come. And other times, it's possible to compromise—which means part of one person's ideas are accepted along with parts of the other person's ideas or that a whole new idea has been accepted.

Today I will look for the good in every person I meet. If I cannot get past their behavior, I will ask God to let me see their 'God-likeness.'

Dear God,

Help me to see the good in everyone. If I cannot agree with another person, then let us agree to disagree but still continue to show respect to each other. Show us that we are all one, Lord.

Thank you, God!

Today I will look for the good in these people:
_____
_____
_____
_____
_____

February 10
FIGHTING

When we fight with our brothers, sisters, or friends, it is usually a verbal battle over something on which we disagree. Fighting is one way in which we learn limits. It is also a way of reacting when we feel thwarted or fearful. Get in touch with what you are feeling. Let your heart be your guide.

If you are unable to work things out verbally, sometimes the fighting becomes physical. Someone may get hurt. Ask yourself if there can be a compromise. For instance, if you both want the same CD or game, could one person have it for 30 minutes and then have it be the other person's turn?

Another solution is to ask for time or space to calm down to think of something that can be done. What other alternatives can you think of to deter a fight?

Today before I allow fighting to turn physical, I will try to calm down and think of alternatives. I will ask for God's help.

Dear God,

Help me to control my anger. Help me to think of alternatives when I am looking for a solution. Remind me to ask for your help to let my love shine through.

Thank you, God!

What are some other things I can do when I feel like fighting?

_____
_____
_____

February 11
LESS IS MORE

The old adage "Less is More" is often very true when it comes to your spiritual life. Less activity in your daily routine means more peace and time for quiet reflection with God. Fewer things to take care of means that you do not become a slave to your belongings and you can appreciate more each item that you do have.

One place in which it is not true, however, is with love. You can never have too much love. And love is something that when overflowing from inside can always be given away.

Today I will not add to my collection of things. Instead I will look to see what I can give away—both in material items and in love.

Dear God,

I want more time to be with you. Help me to get rid of the clutter in my life so that it can happen. With your love flowing through me, I will always have plenty to give away.

Thank you, God!

Things I can give away: _____
_____
_____
_____

Ways I can share the love inside me: _____
_____
_____
_____

February 12
OUTER EXPLORATION

You are beginning to prepare yourself for the adult world and leaving your parents' nurturing. You will want to know more about the world around you. It is a time of testing limits, testing values, and exploring boundaries in the world around you.

This is a difficult time for many parents. In testing limits, you are often stretching or breaking house rules. There is potential danger in outer world exploration. Parents who have loved and nurtured you worry that you may do something that has irreversible consequences. As you get older, this possibility exists because the stakes get higher as you get older. Bad driving choices can result in permanent injury or loss of life. Sexual exploration can result in premature and unwanted pregnancies.

You also are trying to define your own values and code of conduct for yourself. This means that you may question some of your parents' values in the process of evaluating your own. Assure your parents that you love and appreciate them. Let them know you are trying to discover who you are. Ask their patience while you do this.

Today I appreciate my family and continue on my quest to discover who I am.

Dear God,

Thank you for my family. Help me through this time of discovering who I am.

Thank you, God!

Some of my values are: _____
_____
_____

February 13
SHOWING APPRECIATION

Many things are done for us daily by the many people in our lives...the bus driver who sees us safely to and from school, the teacher who teaches us all day, coaches, music instructors, the workers in restaurants, and so on. Many people provide services to us without any acknowledgment.

We can show our appreciation by telling them how much we realize they help us or by just saying "thank you" with a sincere smile. Often just the acknowledgment is enough. Receiving appreciation is one of life's best gifts. For people who really give of themselves, perhaps a gift or card would be the right gesture.

Today I will acknowledge all the people in my life who contribute to my well-being. I will ask God to bless them.

Dear God,

Thank you for all the people who serve me every day. Thanks for people who give of themselves for others as Jesus did. Help me to help others as well. Bless us all.

Thank you, God!

God bless these people!

_____
_____
_____
_____
_____
_____
_____

February 14

ST. VALENTINE'S DAY

St. Valentine's Day is a day to celebrate love. Typically we think of romantic love, as in cupid's arrow striking unsuspecting lovers. We give signs of our love and appreciation in the form of gifts and Valentine cards.

God's love is different. It is unconditional. That means that God loves us just where we are today—without judgment. God is always available to us to give guidance, peace, joy, comfort, and so on. Because of this love for us, God wants only good for us. Sometimes we may make choices that are not in our best interest. God will help to get us back on the right track again.

We can show our love for others, too, by praying for unity and peace throughout the world. Pray that everyone's basic needs will be met. Then get involved in some cause or effort to help others.

Today I pray for a greater love for my fellow human beings.

Dear God,

Help me find a way to express my love for my fellow humans. I pray that we will all unite in harmony and peace. I pray that we all learn unconditional love.

Thank you, God!

A way I can show love to others is (e.g., helping serve meals in a homeless shelter, donating items to the less fortunate, assisting the elderly with difficult chores):

_____
_____
_____

February 15
I AM TIRED OF SCHOOL

Perhaps you are tired of all the homework and tests. You think, "I am tired of school." School is just one way of learning. Even though school is essential to your learning, many of life's lessons are learned outside of the classroom.

Have you ever thought of how much you learn over the summer or when off on a break? Learning continues all of your life. Some learning will be more formal and structured, as in college or classroom work. Other learning will take place through our interaction with others.

Today I see that I will always have learning. I will take it one day at a time and ask God's help in learning my lessons. Here's what I learned today outside of the classroom: _____

_____
_____
_____
_____
_____

Dear God,

Help me to learn my lessons. I appreciate the help of your angels in guiding me. Thank you for all of the challenges and opportunities you set up for me. It makes life exciting always!

Thank you, God!

February 16
KEEPING OUR PERSPECTIVE

What is happiness to you? Sometimes we can be feeling down about something that happened to us—such as an exam we failed. We lose sight of all of the good things that might also have happened that day, and we focus only on the one thing we didn't do so well. We lose our perspective. Suddenly, our little situation or problem becomes a "mountain" of a problem. At these times, we can stop and ask for God's help and redirection. We can take note of all of our blessings.

Today I will not allow small setbacks to let me lose my perspective. I will ask for God's help to remain positive.

Dear God,

Thank you for being there for me through good times and bad. When I start to feel bad about something I've done, help me to redirect my thinking to how I can do better in the future. Help me to acknowledge those things I have done well. Surround me with your grace and love.

Thank you, God!

Good things that happened yesterday and today:

_____
_____
_____
_____
_____
_____

February 17
HONORING LEADERS OF ALL CULTURES

Leaders around the world have the awesome responsibility of maintaining peace and stability among the different cultures. A leader's job can be particularly difficult because there is always someone willing to disagree with the approach being used. It is easy to second-guess a leader. Leaders have to take the risk of trying their plan first. It may look like there is an easy solution, but there seldom is. Most of the time solutions are not black and white, right or wrong, or good and bad. They are just more complicated than they appear on the surface.

Today I will ask God to guide our leaders in making their best decisions. I will respect their willingness to take risks. If I have a constructive suggestion, I will offer it as such.

Dear God,

I give thanks for leaders. I give thanks for their willingness to take risks. I ask your guidance in helping them make decisions for the highest good of their nations. Bring us all to peace and harmony.

Thank you, God!

Write a constructive suggestion and send it to a government representative (local, state, or national). My suggestion is:

_____
_____
_____
_____
_____
_____

February 18
THE MEANING OF LEADERSHIP

Some people might think leadership is about having power or about having important titles and recognition. Leadership is about serving others. A good leader is able to use his or her power in a way that benefits others. Good leaders listen to the people they are serving in order to understand their needs. They are conscientious in taking care of their responsibilities to the people they serve. They act as role models and mentors for others.

There may be times when a leader is questioned or challenged about a decision. Others may disagree, but a good leader will stay with what he or she knows to be the right or true course of action. Leaders need to be courageous and have a good sense of themselves. Otherwise, they will not be able to guide others.

Today I will take stock of my leadership qualities. What quality do I need to develop? _____
_____
_____
_____

How can I support good leaders? _____
_____
_____
_____

Dear God,

Thank you for good leaders. Help me to know the difference between a leader who is using his or her power for good and one who is not. Teach me leadership skills.

Thank you, God!

February 19

FINDING OUT WHO WE ARE

The question, "Who am I?" might be more accurate as, "Who am I right now?" That's because you are always changing as you grow. Take a sheet of paper and write down what you like to do...hobbies, interests, friends, talents...and also write down what you are good at doing and what you want to improve. Include what you believe in or anything about which you are unsure. If you keep a daily journal, or even if you write in it only weekly, you will be able to see yourself grow.

Every year it would be helpful to assess how you've grown. What skills have you gained since last year, and what goals have you made for next year? _____
_____
_____
_____

Today I will appreciate the person I am right now, knowing that God loves me just as I am.

Dear God,

Help me to know myself—my strengths and weaknesses. Help me to celebrate the things I do well and strengthen those things I do not do as well. Thank you, God, for helping me see myself through your eyes.

Thank you, God!

February 20

PATIENCE (BEING GENTLE WITH MYSELF AND OTHERS)

Patience is being gentle with yourself and others and allowing the time required for whatever you or they are doing. It is as easy to be impatient with yourself as with others. Perhaps you are not learning a task or lesson as fast as you think you should. Listen to you talking to yourself. Do you berate yourself, call yourself names?

When you learn to treat yourself with courtesy, respect, and patience, then you will find it easier to treat others in the same way.

Today I will treat myself with gentleness and respect. I will work on being patient with myself and others.

Dear God,

Sometimes I am the hardest on myself. Help me to work on being kinder and more patient with myself and others.

Thank you, God!

Here is how I am being gentle with myself and others:

_____
_____
_____
_____
_____

February 21

NEGATIVE FEELINGS AND THINKING

Negative feelings can surround us from the moment we wake up. Feelings of doubt about ourselves or negative feelings regarding how the day will go or how we will be accepted and so on can seem to come from inside us.

We can choose to act from the fear coming from inside of us or we can choose to think positive thoughts. Look into the mirror as you tell yourself: "I will do well today," "Everything will go smoothly today," "I will be able to handle anything that happens today with God's help. I do not need to fear." These are examples of affirmations that you can say to set your thinking on a positive note.

Today I will choose not to act from fear. Today I choose to think positive thoughts about myself and others. I choose to look for the good in everyone and everything that happens.

Dear God,

I want to see the good in myself. Help me to imagine how I want things to happen today and then to make a positive statement as to how I see the situation or event unfolding. Help me to transform my life through thinking positively.

Thank you, God!

How I want to act today: _____
_____
_____
_____

A positive statement I can say to myself every day is:
_____

February 22
POSITIVE THINKING

Learning to think positively is a lifelong process. It is easy to see the bad side of something that happens. It takes effort to look at the positive side. If you always think negatively, that is what you focus on and it will continue to dominate your life and make you feel sad and depressed. If you think positively or try to see the good side of something, your focus will be on your 'good.' For example, if you fail a test, the negative way to look at it might be, "I'm stupid. I don't know anything. I'm a failure." This does not do a lot for your self-esteem and does not change your habits to improve in the future.

The positive way is to say, "I didn't do well today. How might I improve my study habits so I can do better in the future?" This statement accepts the bad score as only temporary and then looks for ways to improve.

Today I will listen to my self-talk. If I make a negative statement, I will immediately think of the positive side so I can retrain my thoughts.

Dear God,

I know I have control over my thoughts. Help me to train myself to think in a positive, nurturing way so I can grow and be a model for others.

Thank you, God!

A positive, nurturing thought I can repeat to myself is:

_____
_____
_____

February 23
LETTING GO

When something has happened that you feel you cannot handle, turn it over to God. Once you place it in God's care, you no longer need to worry. Things will just be taken care of by God.

Create a "God" jar or box. Have fun decorating it. Write down the concern you have and place it in the jar or box. Then allow for everything to just fall in place. Ask God to have everything work out for your highest good. Then thank God and do not think about it anymore. Let go of any expectations you might have about how it will turn out.

Today I will turn my problem over to God and let go of it.

Dear God,

I place this problem in your hands and ask that it be worked out for my highest good and for the highest good of everyone involved. Help me to let go of the outcome and trust in your love and care.

Thank you, God!

I will put these concerns in my "God" jar:
_____
_____
_____

February 24
SETTING GOALS

If we want to know which way we are going, we must set goals. Goals should state what we want the outcome to be. For instance, I might set a goal of exhibiting my animal at the State Fair. In order for that to happen, I will need to join a local club where I can learn animal care and compete for the privilege of exhibiting my animal at the State Fair. I might also need to save up money to spend at the Fair and arrange transportation for my animal and myself, and so on. Perhaps we might need some adult coaching to make sure we have covered everything. Once we set goals, the actions will become clear.

What goals might you set for yourself now? Is there something you want to learn to do? Somewhere you want to go? Be sure your goals are achievable. _____
_____
_____

What steps will you need to get there?
1. _____
2. _____
3. _____
4. _____

Goals are something you will be setting for the rest of your life. They help you to grow.

Today I will set some goals for myself and work out the actions required.

Dear God,

Help me to set goals that are good for me and will help me grow.

Thank you, God!

February 25

Today
I feel gratitude
growing
in my heart
for all
blessings
that God
has given me.

Thank you, God!

February 26
LIVING IN THE PRESENT MOMENT

Sometimes we are worried about a test in the future, or other times our thoughts dwell on something we already did that cannot be changed. By having our thoughts in the past or future, we miss the present moment. Life is lived in the present. Only what you do today can affect the future. The past cannot be changed.

To live in the present moment is to be aware of everything and everyone around you. See, smell, taste, touch, and hear everything around you. Take the time to appreciate what you have.

Today I will take a walk in nature. I will find a spot on a log or on soft grass to just be aware of everything around me. I will write down my observations. What did I learn?

_____
_____
_____
_____
_____

Dear God,

Sometimes we become so caught up in being busy that we miss 'life' around us. Help us to take the time to appreciate and learn from your Creation surrounding us in this moment.

Thank you, God!

February 27
MAKING A DIFFERENCE

Each person is born with unique talents and gifts from God. We each have the power within us to make a difference in our world. Whether it is to lift up and comfort someone else, to make the world more beautiful by planting trees and flowers, or to make changes in the way our society operates, we can all make a difference.

What have you done to make your world a better place? Think of two new things you can do to improve it, and start working on them today.

_____
_____
_____
_____

Today I will become a contributing member of my world. I will personally help to make it a better place because of me.

Dear God,

Thy will be done. Where do you need me most to make a difference? Inspire me with energy and enthusiasm to get it done.

Thank you, God!

February 28

OWNING YOUR INNER POWER

Inner power comes from believing you can do it. To own your inner power, you must believe in yourself. If you say, "I can't do that," or if you think someone else can do it better than you, you are not owning your own power.

You can do anything you set your mind to do!! Believe in yourself! Use positive thought patterns: "I can do it!" or "I will do it!" or "I am doing it!" As always, start with one step at a time. The more you do, the more you know you can do. Build your own confidence by getting started now.

Today I will believe in myself and my ability to move mountains one step at a time. I do not have to do it alone...God is with me, just by my asking.

Dear God,

With you as my partner, I can do anything! Help me to develop my own inner power.

Thank you, God!

The first three steps I can take toward what I want to do—with God's help—are:
1. _____
2. _____
3. _____

March 1

THE POWER OF PRAYER

Jesus said, "Whenever two or more are gathered in my name, there I am also." Scientists have been able to measure the energy of people praying or thinking good thoughts. They found it to be the power of the group squared when the group was totally in agreement in its intention.[2] This means that when a group gets together for a good purpose, their energy can be squared by the number participating.

Your thoughts are prayers. If you think of someone who needs help or you have kind thoughts about another, this is prayer. Anything that comes from the heart is prayer. Miracles occur when concerned family members pray for a loved one who is ill.

So whenever you have a concern for which you wish to pray, grab another person or several persons to pray with you. Be clear in your intention.

Today I will think positive thoughts and know they are prayers. If I have an important concern, I will ask others to pray with me.

Dear God,
I know I do not need to use fancy words to pray. You see what is in my heart. Help me to see you through my prayers.

Thank you, God!

Today I pray for: _____
_____
_____

March 2
HURT FEELINGS

Sometimes I get my feelings hurt. My friend may not even know he or she did something that hurt me. I accept that I am in control of my responses. I will look for the truth in the situation and ask for God's help in understanding it. At these times, I need to try to understand why I felt hurt and why I need to be forgiving.

Today I will work on trying to understand my emotions and why I respond the way I do. If I am unclear, I will try to write it out on paper or talk it over with a friend. The answers are all inside me; I need to take the time to figure it out.

Dear God,

Help me to understand my own emotions and feelings. Help me to develop a forgiving heart and to try to be understanding when others' feelings get hurt.

Thank you, God!

Feelings I have and what I think they mean:
_____
_____
_____
_____

March 3

*Today
I surrender
to God's Plan
for me.
I trust
in God's goodness.*

Thank you, God!

March 4
ACCEPTING MY BODY

You gave me a gift when you gave me my body, God! Sometimes I compare my body to the body of others and I see something I wish was different. Right now my body is changing a lot as I grow. These changes are hard to accept. I have a hard time seeing my body for the miracle that it is. It is able to operate even when I am not conscious of it. It can give me energy to do things and heal itself if it gets injured. My body gives me freedom to move around, run, dance, and experience life.

Today I will give thanks for the miracle of my body. I will look in a mirror and tell myself "I love you."

Dear God,

Help me to be grateful for my body. Help me to accept what I have as something unique to me and to look for the beautiful spirit within me.

Thank you, God!

Things I like about my body:
_____
_____
_____
_____
_____

March 5
ACCEPTING MYSELF

Accepting ourselves is one of the hardest things to do. We are all on a spiritual journey whether we realize it or not. We are precious children to God, and God is helping us to grow and build character by presenting different lessons for us to learn. As we master them, we go on to another lesson. The people around us often act as mirrors of the behavior we do not like to see in ourselves. Rather than condemn others' behavior, we need to reflect on how what we are witnessing relates to us. We are all learning at our own rate. So it is senseless to worry over how others are doing, because they are developing at their own rate, too.

All we need to do is to become more aware of what we are thinking, feeling, and doing. Is what we are doing what God would want us to do? Is it for the good of ourselves and everyone around us? Along with God being our best friend, we can be our own best friend.

Today I will be my own best friend. I will think good things about myself and tell myself I am loved by God so I can love myself.

Dear God,

Sometimes I do not appreciate myself. I think about all the things I do wrong instead of thinking about how much I do right. Guide me to be my own best friend and to love myself as you love me.

Thank you, God!

Good things I like about myself:
_____
_____
_____

March 6
DEALING WITH ILLNESS

Severe illness sometimes occurs in teens and children. Maybe you know someone who has a serious illness. What can you say to someone who is very ill? This situation is something that makes everyone feel uncomfortable. Because we feel uncomfortable, the tendency is to pull away. Instead, the person needs to feel our love and caring.

Pray to God for the wisdom to understand what is happening and what we are to learn from this. Bring magazines, toys, and games to help keep him or her be entertained. Joke and try to be light in your conversation as much as possible. Sometimes, you will not have to say anything. Just being at the person's side will be enough. Make cards that show your love. Pray that the very best will happen for the person and that the best doctors and specialists will be there to help. Then pray to accept God's will.

Today I will be there for anyone who is suffering from severe illness.

Dear God,

It is hard to understand severe illness in children and teens. I pray that your will be done and that they be supported by those who care about them. I also pray that the best doctors and specialists help them.

Thank you, God!

People facing illness for whom I now pray:
_____
_____
_____

March 7
CHOOSING TO BE A FRIEND

Friends are precious gifts from God. When you are a good friend to others, you will influence others to be a good friend to you.

Sometimes people have trouble making friends. Perhaps they have problems at home or do not feel good about themselves. You can help them to be a friend. First, smile at them even when they are unkind to you. Accept them as they are. Do not judge them. Focus on what you like about them. If it helps, picture Jesus behind them and pretend you are talking to him. Do an unexpected kindness for them. Soon you will find them becoming your friends.

Sometimes if a friend is not well-liked, others may try to convince you to not be his or her friend anymore. Help the others to see the good in your friend also.

Today I will be the best friend I can be to myself and others. I will do an unexpected kindness for someone who is giving me trouble.

Dear God,

Help me to model being a good friend. Thanks for being my best friend, God. Help me to be kind even when I do not feel like it.

Thank you, God!

Ways I choose to be a friend today:
_____
_____
_____
_____

March 8
LOYALTY

When you are loyal to someone, you align yourself with that person. You believe what he or she believes and develop a trust with the person. You do not talk about the person or his or her secrets to anyone else without permission. Being loyal is about trusting and believing in the other person.

If we are Christians, we are loyal to God and Jesus. We believe the truths taught to us by Jesus and try to model our behavior to reflect those beliefs. It is a trust that we develop between ourselves and God.

Today my behavior will model the loyalty I feel to God, my Creator. I will show by my example the teachings of Jesus Christ.

Dear God,

You have always been loyal to your people. Help me to model that loyalty back to you through my thoughts, words, and actions.

Thank you, God!

Ways I can show my loyalty to God today:

_____
_____
_____
_____

March 9
BEING A TEAM PLAYER

Being a team player means that you are willing to do your part to bring out the group's highest performance. It means that sometimes you will be willing to give up the need for you to shine as an individual in order to see the entire group do its best.

By being a team player at school or in your class, it means you are willing to do whatever is best for the whole. At home, it means that you are willing to do whatever is the highest good for your family, even if it's not exactly what you might want to do.

Today I will look for whatever is the highest good of the group of which I am a part. I will make decisions based on the good of the entire group—not just myself.

Dear God,

Help me to see the highest good for my group or family. Help me to be selfless in my actions if it is the best for everyone else.

Thank you, God!

Actions I can take today as a team player:
_____
_____
_____
_____

March 10
LOOKING FOR THE GOOD IN OTHERS

Often it is difficult to see the good in someone else when we are focusing on something we do not like. Is there someone you do not particularly like? Ask God to help you to see the good in that person. Write down the good things you have seen in him or her:

_____
_____

Try to focus on those qualities.

You will begin to notice more and more good qualities once you change your focus to the good. The trouble is that we often focus on the things that aggravate us, thereby bringing more of the same to us.

Today I will focus on the good in others. I will not participate in gossip or any behavior that will bring another's bad qualities into focus.

Dear God,

Help me to train my focus to be on the good in others, as you have been able to see the good in me.

Thank you, God!

March 11

*Today I feel the love
and light of God
flowing through me...
surrounding everyone
who comes near my path.*

*Thank you,
God!*

March 12

DETERMINING STRENGTHS AND WEAKNESSES

When we bring home our report card, it is easy to see where our strengths are: our best grades or the subjects we like the best. We also need to take a look at our personal strengths. Do we get along well with others? Do we give of our time and talents to others, or do we think we do not have anything to offer?

Do we have a good feeling of our self-worth, or do we think someone else is always better than we are. Take the time to write down your strengths, and then run them by someone who knows you well, such as a parent or friend. See if they agree or can think of any others.

Then do the same with your weaknesses. What do you need to work on? Just because you have a bad temper or are impatient, it does not mean you will always be that way. You are always growing. If you decide to change, you will.

Today I will take a look at my strengths and weaknesses. I will look at my strengths and determine how I can use them to serve myself and others. Then I will look at my weaknesses and choose one that I am willing to work on to improve.

Dear God,

I know that I am always changing and growing. Help me to change myself for the better.

Thank you, God!

Strengths I see in myself: _____

Weaknesses I'd like to strengthen: _____

March 13
WORTHINESS

Worthiness has to do with how you feel about yourself. Do you believe in yourself, or do you believe everyone else is smarter, funnier, and more talented than you? God has given each person unique talents. Every person is of value to God. No one is better than or of lesser value than another. See yourself as a person of worth.

Become a cheerleader for yourself. Say "I can do it! I can do it!" and then believe it. Try new things. The more experiences you have, the more confidence you will have. Confidence brings along with it higher feelings of competence and self-worth.

Today I will try new experiences and be my own cheerleader. I can do anything I set my mind to do!

Dear God,

Help me to develop a high sense of self-worth. Help me to see myself as you see me.

Thank you, God!

New experiences I will try: _____

_____
_____
_____
_____

March 14
WHAT AM I BEST AT DOING?

You are always learning new things while you are in school. What you are best at doing may still be developing. Perhaps your gift is being a good listener for others. Maybe you are the leader or a good team player. When arguments arise, you may be the peacemaker or mediator. Young people are in the process of becoming. You are capable of being much more than you are now.

Ask God to help you discover what your talents are and how you may use them to help others.

Today I will take a good look at myself to see where I might be good at helping others.

Dear God,

Help me to discover what my best talents are for helping myself and others. Help me to develop those talents to their best use.

Thank you, God!

Talents I think I have: _____
_____
_____
_____

March 15
BEING A GOOD SPORT

Being a good sport means that you are able to behave courteously to others even when you are not winning. When someone else wins, you say "Good game" or "You played well." When you win, you do not gloat or tell the other person he or she is a loser; instead just say "Thanks! You played a good game" or "I enjoyed playing against you." This makes others feel good about themselves even if they did not win. Next time they will want to play with you again.

Games and sports soon become no fun when people are so competitive that they place winning the game over showing respect and courtesy toward their opponent.

Today I will be a good sport in any sport or games I play. I will always show respect to my opponent. However, I will give it my best effort.

Dear God,

Help me to be a good sport. Let me never lose sight of my need to respect others and consider their feelings.

Thank you, God!

Ways I can respect others today:
_____
_____
_____
_____

March 16
RECYCLING

By recycling papers, plastics, cans, and so on, we are helping to reduce the waste being dumped into the earth. In the last 100 years, we have dramatically increased the amount of trash dumped. If we keep dumping trash like that, what will happen to the earth? Will we all be living on landfills? We can help too by recycling toys, games, clothes, and anything that is not completely worn out or useless. We can also take better care of what we own so that it lasts longer.

Find out what your community is doing to recycle. Help your parents to recycle. When you clean your room out and have outgrown games, give them to a charity organization that will distribute them to be reused.

The other thing you can do is to ask yourself when you want to buy something, "Do I really need this or do I just want this?"

Today I will become involved in recycling and learn more about what I can do to reduce, reuse, and recycle.

Dear God,

Help me to become a good caretaker of the earth. Help me to reuse and reduce the items I have that I no longer need. Help me to take care of what I have so it will last longer.

Thank you, God!

Things I can recycle or donate: _____
_____
_____
_____
_____

March 17

HONORING ST. PATRICK

St. Patrick was a missionary priest who spent over 40 years in Ireland converting the people to Christianity. He preached; baptized; and established churches, schools, and colleges. March 17th is celebrated in Ireland to honor and remember him. This holiday is also celebrated in the United States because of all the Irish immigrants who live here.

St. Patrick used the shamrock when teaching the Holy Trinity: Father, Son, and Holy Spirit. Since then the shamrock has become the symbol of the land of Ireland.

Today I will honor St. Patrick, using his good works as a model for my behavior.

Dear God,

Help me to live my life as an example to others. Help me to serve through the gifts and talents I have to offer.

Thank you, God!

Ways I can honor St. Patrick and other missionaries today:

_____
_____
_____
_____
_____

March 18

WHAT DO I WANT TO BE WHEN I GROW UP?

Finding out what you want to be when you grow up requires some research, and your ideas may change many times before you actually get there. The first thing you need to do is to identify those things you really like to do. Do you like to work with others or alone? What do you enjoy doing? If you think you might be interested in a certain type of work, talk to people who do it. What do they like about it or dislike? What did they have to do to prepare for that career? What are you good at doing? Write down your thoughts about this.

As a person goes through life, his or her work may change. Everything you do will provide skills for the next job. Just work to build your skills and confidence. God will provide the opportunities once you decide what you want to do.

Today I will think about my skills and talents and what I might enjoy doing. Then I will talk to someone who is doing that kind of work.

Dear God,

Help me to choose a career that suits my talents and helps others. No matter what I do, Lord, help me to do my best. Guide me to learn what I need to prepare for my adult work.

Thank you, God!

What are my talents? _____
_____
_____
_____

March 19
FEELING INFERIOR

It is easy to feel inferior if you compare yourself to others. Other people may have had experiences you haven't had, and they may be developing at a different rate. Do not compare! You are a unique person developing at your own rate. You will have experiences at different times than others, and you may have some experiences that they do not have. Learn to appreciate and celebrate your uniqueness. What do you have to offer the group or your friends? For instance, are you a good listener, note taker, easy to be around?

If you are feeling low about yourself, ask God to help you see your true gifts. Then call a friend and spend the day having fun together. It will lift your spirit.

Today I will celebrate my uniqueness. I will not compare myself to others. I will celebrate the uniqueness of others too.

Dear God,

Thank you for helping me see my true gifts. Thank you for others who appreciate me. Help me to appreciate myself!

Thank you, God!

Ways I am unique:_____
_____
_____

Ways others I know are unique: _____
_____
_____

March 20

WHEN IT'S SPRING, THERE IS HOPE

After a long winter, when everything looks dead and you wonder if you could possibly see something green again, spring arrives and life bursts forth with extra vigor—bringing hope for renewal of earth and spirit. The sun becomes more intense and the air smells more fragrant.

Life is often like this too. When things have conspired to make your outlook bleak, suddenly there is a change of events. Everything begins to look sweeter and more hopeful. Keeping "hope" alive keeps your spirit alive.

Today I will celebrate the arrival of spring and the revival of the hope of good things to come.

Dear God,

Thank you for the renewal of spring...the greening of lawns and trees, the colorful flowers, the buzzing of bees in pollination. Help me to always remember the hope you give us that our good is waiting to come to us. Help me to never lose hope!

Thank you, God!

Here's what I think about spring: _____
_____
_____
_____

March 21
ASKING FOR GUIDANCE

We get confused sometimes and do not know what to do. This is when we need to turn to God for guidance. God will put the right people in front of us to help solve the problem or give us guidance. We can also use prayer and meditation to connect to God's inspiration.

Life can be overwhelming if you think you have to solve everything yourself. We are all here to help each other. On the other hand, once guidance comes to us, we can choose whether to accept it. That's God's gift to us.

Today I will ask God's help in figuring out how to solve my problems.

Dear God,

Thank you for the help you give to me when I ask. I know you will always be there for me.

Thank you, God!

I can ask God for guidance with these concerns:

_____
_____
_____
_____
_____

March 22
FEELING SECURE

We feel secure in knowing that our parents love us. We feel secure knowing food will be on the table and a roof will protect us from the elements. God is available to everyone whether their behavior is good or bad. God takes care of the birds of the air, the animals of the forest, and the fish of the sea. We are made in God's image, and God wants to take care of us too if we will allow it. But, because of the gift of free choice, sometimes we do not let God take care of us.

If we grow in faith with God, we will always feel secure in the knowledge that God will be there to aid us if we run into difficulties.

Today I feel secure knowing that God is my partner in life. God is always there—when I know I need help and even when I don't realize I need help.

Dear God,

Help me to grow in faith with you and to be secure in the knowledge that you are always there for me when I need you.

Thank you, God!

These are ways I feel secure: _____
_____
_____
_____
_____

March 23
COUNTING OUR BLESSINGS

When we focus on our blessings, we do not have time to think about what is wrong with our life. In truth, we are unaware of many of the gifts God gives to us...especially the unseen ones.

Grab a piece of paper and begin writing down some of your blessings. If you do it over a day or two, some ideas you had not thought of will come to you. Take time in your heart to give thanks to God.

Exercise: Have every member of your family write down one thing they appreciate about each member of the family. Then share the ideas with each other. Many times it will be a surprise to find what others appreciate about you.

Today I will focus on the blessings of my life.

Dear God,

You are so good to me. I do not even know all of the ways you have been good to me. Give me a greater awareness of my blessings.

Thank you, God!

Blessings I count today: _____
_____
_____
_____
_____
_____

March 24
USING MANNERS

Etiquette is a word that describes a standard of behavior used between people to show respect. Expressions such as, "May I help you?" "Thank you." "It's nice to meet you." and "Excuse me" are all used to smooth relations between people and to show respect. Opening a door for someone, pulling out a chair for someone, or helping an older person are all ways of showing we love our neighbors as ourselves.

When someone says such things as, "Hey, stupid!" or "Shut up," the tone changes and neither the tone nor the words show respect.

Today I will learn good manners as a tool in helping me get along with others and show respect.

Dear God,

Help me to learn the right words to bring peaceful relationships into my life. Help me to show respect to myself and others.

Thank you, God!

Good manners I can use today: _____
_____
_____
_____
_____
_____
_____

March 25

ADDRESSING SENIORS WITH RESPECT

By saying "Mr." or "Mrs." before someone's name, you are showing respect. "Sir" or "Ma'am" are also acceptable substitutes. You would usually address a teacher or friend of your parents this way unless they give you permission to use their more familiar name. You might ask them how they would like you to address them.

In today's society, with stepparents and other changes in family, some forms of courtesy are not being used. Accordingly, the show of respect is being lost, too. Good manners are never old-fashioned. Older people have a lot of life experience and wisdom to give to us. They should be shown respect.

Today I will address my seniors with proper courtesy as a show of my respect for them.

Dear God,

It's easy to think I'm so smart that I do not have to answer to anyone or that older people can't teach me anything. When I think that way, I am only showing how much I really need to learn. Help me to be humble and treat my elders with respect and courtesy.

Thank you, God!

How I address the older people in my life:_____
_____
_____
_____
_____
_____

March 26
COMMUNICATING

Sometimes we come home from school and want to get together with a friend. We fool around for a while, and by the time we call, our friend is already doing something else. This translates into lost opportunity and often makes us sad. The lost opportunity could be in telling another how much you love and appreciate him or her or that you forgive the person for something he or she did to you. If that is not communicated, it can forever stand between you. It could also be lost opportunity for things you would like to do or accomplish. The more you communicate, the better your opportunities and relationships will be.

Today I will focus on my communications. I will allow God to be my guide.

Dear God,

Please help me to better communicate my feelings and goals to myself and others.

Thank you, God!

Feelings and goals I can communicate today: _____
_____
_____
_____
_____
_____
_____

March 27

Today
I am trusting
my inner voice
and
inner wisdom.

Thank you, God!

March 28

PASSOVER

Passover is a very important holiday in the Jewish faith. It commemorates the time when God helped free the Jews from slavery under Rameses II's Egyptian rule. The 10 plagues visited upon the Egyptians when Rameses II refused to let the Jews go are documented in Exodus in the Bible.

When all the first-born males were ordered killed, God instructed all Jews to put the blood of a lamb on their doors. All the Jewish homes were "passed over," and the Jewish people were unharmed. When the Egyptians chased the Jews into the desert, the Red Sea parted for the Jews to cross. The Red Sea closed again as the Egyptians pursued. God asked the Jews to pray for their enemies.

The Jews were in such a rush to leave Egypt that they had no time to bake bread. Instead, they ate matzo, an unleavened bread. During Passover, certain foods are prepared in a special way. Seder is the name of the Passover feast, which is celebrated for 8 days in late March or early April. Prayers are read from the Haggadah; songs are sung, and the story of Passover is read and remembered.

Today I will befriend someone who is Jewish and ask what Passover means to him or her.

Dear God,

You are with us always through our trials and tribulations. Just as you helped the Jewish people be freed, help me have the faith that it took for the Jews to be freed from their slavery.

Thank you, God!

I have faith that with God I can overcome:

_____

March 29

JESUS' TRIALS AND FORGIVENESS

When Jesus went through his trials, he offered no resistance. He knew he would die for voicing his truth, but he could not do otherwise. Jesus asked, "Father, forgive them for they do not know what they do." Even as the soldiers pierced his breast with a sword, he forgave them.

We are called to do the same...forgive our enemies—forgive and look for the lesson we are to learn.

Today as I reflect on the life of Jesus, I will ask God for forgiveness and the courage to forgive my enemies as Jesus did.

Dear God,

Sometimes when I get very angry, the last thing I feel like doing is forgiving. Help me to remember Jesus and his ability to forgive. Give me a loving and compassionate heart so I may forgive my enemies too.

Thank you, God!

Today I forgive (e.g., Linda, for calling me a name):
I forgive _____ for _____.
I forgive _____ for _____.
I forgive _____ for _____.
I forgive _____ for _____.

March 30
GOING TO EXTREMES

It is wise to live moderately. For example, if your mother bakes a pie, having a nice piece is an example of living moderately. Eating the whole pie in one sitting might be considered extreme. This is true whether it concerns food, getting enough sleep, having too many games or CDs, or throwing temper tantrums.

Picture a ruler; think of the right side of the ruler representing "too much" and the left side "too little." The midpoint would be "just right." The midpoint then represents living moderately or living in balance.

Now think about yourself. Do you allow yourself to get overly tired and cranky? Where would that be on the ruler? Do you play so hard that you forget to eat or tell your mother where you are? Where would that be on the ruler? Are you so concerned with popular trends that you go out of your way to get something even though you don't need it? Where would that be on the ruler?

Today I will examine my life to see where I might be living in extremes.

Dear God,

Help me to find the balance in my life. I want to do your will. Help me to see those areas I need to work on.

Thank you, God!

Ways I can find the "balance" today: _____
_____
_____
_____

March 31

THE PROMISE OF EASTER

Through his death on the cross, Jesus modeled for us the fact that his spirit lives on. He came back and appeared to the disciples to prove that he never really left and that he will be with us always, any time we need him. His spirit is eternal just as is ours. When our body dies, we cross over into the spirit world and are one with God again.

Easter is a celebration of hope. It signifies the hope of life eternal and the hope of Spring yet to come. The Easter egg is used by some people as a symbol of new life.

Today I give thanks for my eternal spirit and for hope of life yet to come.

Dear God,

I've always been afraid of death, but Jesus shows us we have nothing to fear. Our soul lives on with you.

Thank you, God!

What Easter means to me: _____
_____
_____
_____

April 1
APRIL FOOL'S DAY

April Fool's Day is a day when young people and adults enjoy playing tricks on each other. We like to pretend that something is different than it really is. It is representative of the illusion in which we truly live.

The way we perceive our life is often far from the truth. For example, Johnny is afraid of the dark. He says he sees and hears monsters. Are there really monsters? No—but Johnny believes they are there, so for him they exist. Both young people and adults have fears that represent their "monster." The monsters keep them from seeing the truth until they are able to get through their fears. Then there are no longer any monsters. Where do you have "monster" fears? List them here:

_____
_____
_____
_____
_____
_____

Today I will look at any fears I have that keep me from seeing the truth of my being.

Dear God,

Help me to see the fears that mask my truth. I choose to let go of them. Give me courage to get past my fears.

Thank you, God!

April 2
CAUGHT BEING BAD

Sometimes I am caught being bad. I do not feel good about myself when this happens. I know I can do better. God will help me to learn from my mistakes. God loves me just the way I am. God can help me anytime I ask for help to get in touch with my feelings and to make choices that are in my best interest. I must remember that I am learning and forgive myself for any misjudgments I make. If I have done anything to hurt another, I will ask forgiveness and restore the person's property or friendship.

I forgive myself for:

_____
_____
_____
_____

Today I will forgive myself for any mistakes I make and ask God's help in making good choices.

Dear God,

Sometimes I lose sight of my own goodness. When I do, please help me to forgive myself and make better choices the next time.

Thank you, God!

April 3

Isaiah 11:6

The wolf shall dwell with the lamb, and the leopard shall lie down with the kid, and the calf and the lion and the fatling together, and a little child shall lead them.

Thank you, God!

April 4
LOOKING FOR THE GOOD IN EVERYTHING

Sometimes the world can look pretty bad when we witness the crimes being committed and reported on the news. God has a way of setting up circumstances for everyone to learn something. We learn something by witnessing it. The people involved also learn about forgiveness or how they feel when they do something bad to another person and what those consequences might be.

Maybe you have to move to another city and you feel that it is terrible. However, God may bless you with a great new school and a best friend that you are delighted to have. Give each situation a chance to develop and have faith that God will work for your good.

By looking for the good or gift in every situation, you will be more likely to find it.

Today I will look for the good or gift in every situation. I will not dwell on bad things that happen.

Dear God,

Help me to see the good or gift in everything that happens.

Thank you, God!

These are situations in which I am looking for the good:

_____
_____
_____
_____

April 5
DOING CHORES

Doing chores usually involves doing small tasks around the house, which helps the family. Everyone in the family contributes to the need to care for the home and its occupants. By sharing in these tasks, you gain knowledge of how to take care of yourself. You gain self-confidence. The more you do, the more you know you can do if the need arises.

Sometimes chores can feel like a drag. They get in the way of having fun, but they can also teach you follow-through. The best idea is to think of a way to make chores fun. Or plan to do them at a time when they will not get in the way of fun. This means you need to *plan* to make them a part of your day. Do not just leave them to be done when it becomes convenient. That time may never happen.

Today I will plan when to do chores so they will not get in the way of the fun things I want to do.

Dear God,

Help me to see my chores as part of my growing up experience. When they do not seem like fun, help me think of ways to make them more fun or to just daydream through them.

Thank you, God!

Chores I plan to do today and when I plan to do them:
_____
_____
_____
_____

April 6
TRYING NEW THINGS

Trying something new can be scary or it can be fun. It may offer us gifts we never imagined. However, if we are too afraid to try it, then we miss the opportunity. For example, learning to ride a bike can be scary. You can fall down and hurt yourself. However, once riding your bike is mastered, you can go a far greater distance than if you had to walk. Bike rides with friends can be lots of fun. Riding a bike also offers a fun way to exercise and develop the muscles in your legs.

Trying new foods can be difficult, too, but by doing this you may find new foods you really like. The more you are willing to try new things, the greater your horizons or possibilities will be. A person open to new ideas might travel to a foreign country and experience many new ways of living.

Today I will open my horizons by trying something new.

Dear God,

Help me to stay open to the opportunities you put before me. Then help me to choose the things I will take for myself. May my actions always be acceptable to you.

Thank you, God!

New things I will try today: _____
_____
_____
_____

April 7

FEELING GOOD ABOUT YOURSELF WITHOUT PUTTING OTHERS DOWN

So much of the time in school you are competing against other students. In the process of that competition, you are forced to see how you measure up against others. It is important to recognize your accomplishments and what you are learning even though you may not do as well as someone else. Once in a while you may win the top honor, though. When you do, it is important to focus only on your accomplishments and not on what others did not do.

You do not look better by making others look worse. On the contrary, it takes away from your achievement when you diminish someone else. Instead, focus on your achievement and thank all those who helped you get there.

Today I will focus on my achievements, whether they are at the top or not. What others do will not be my concern, except to recognize them and be happy when they do well too.

Dear God,

Thank you for my successes. Help me to develop a grateful attitude toward those who help me succeed. Let me never put anyone else down in my effort to look good.

Thank you, God!

What I can do well today: _____
_____
_____
_____

April 8
BOREDOM

Once in a while we have some plans change or maybe the weather gets in the way. Then we have some unexpected time to fill. If we dwell on the time that needs to be filled or if the activity being suggested is not to our liking, we might feel bored. Actually, we are choosing to be bored.

Yes, it is a choice. Ask God to bring to your mind some thoughts of things to do. You will have plenty of ideas from which to choose. Invite a friend over or do a puzzle; write a story or paint a picture; listen to music; read a book; take a walk; ride your bike; or play cards. It is your choice to fill your time or not to fill your time with meaningful activity.

Today I will choose to be happy and fill my time with creative, meaningful activities.

Dear God,

When I am being bored, remind me to ask you for ways to fill my time. Let me not burden others with a sad face. I know I can handle this myself.

Thank you, God!

How I choose to fill my free time today:

_____
_____
_____
_____

April 9
WHEN AM I MAKING A GOOD DECISION?

There are several ways to know if you are making a good decision. Ask yourself: (1) Does it hurt you or anyone else? (2) What will happen when you make this decision? (3) What is the possible outcome? Ask God's guidance. Many times we make decisions on impulse and then just pay consequences later. This might work when you are younger, but as you get older, the consequences of your decisions can be life threatening.

Before you make any decision, give yourself time to think of consequences. You might even have to "sleep on it." If you feel comfortable with a friend or an adult, ask what he or she thinks. This will help you make a more informed decision.

Today I will take time to think of consequences before making a decision concerning something I want to do. I will pray for God's guidance.

Dear God,

I need your help in making decisions. I am new to this process. I do not want to hurt myself or anyone else. Give me the wisdom and judgment to make good decisions.

Thank you, God!

Decisions I am facing: _____
_____
_____
_____
_____

April 10

CARE OF YOUR BELONGINGS

Taking care of your belongings makes them last longer. It also means putting them in a place where you can find them when you need them.

We are all blessed with the belongings God gives us. We honor God when we show respect and take care of those things.

We should get only as much as we really need or for which we are willing to care. Do you have items that get lost in your room because you have too many things? Go through your things and sort out those items you are willing to give away. Not only will you be recycling your things, but you will also be lightening the amount of things you will have to take care of.

Today I will take care of my possessions and will sort out those items I no longer need.

Dear God,

I am grateful for all those things that you give me. Help me to take care of them and to not take more than I need.

Thank you, God!

Time today when I will sort through my things and choose items to give away: _____

April 11
THE TRUE VALUE OF OUR THINGS

We often attach great value to things we own. Sometimes we even get confused and value our things over people. In truth, possessions may come and go. They wear out or get lost, or we lose interest in them. People, shared experiences with friends, and good memories have more value. They stay with us when possessions fade away. People can love us back and teach us things. Possessions just sit there collecting dust and taking up space.

Possessions can become a barrier to us moving on in our growth when we have to focus too much care and attention on them. They can become time consuming and feel like a noose around our neck.

Today I will take a close look at my possessions. Am I owning them or are they owning me? I will recycle anything I no longer need.

Dear God,

Help me to see what part my possessions play in my life. Help me to value them for the tools they are. Let me never value them over people.

Thank you, God!

The things I value are:_____
_____
_____
_____
_____

April 12
SHOWING RESPECT FOR EACH OTHER

When we show respect for each other, it means we treat each other as we would like to be treated. We do not push, shove, or gossip about another person. We do not exclude another from activities with other friends. We do not call names or try to get another in trouble.

When we are kind, loving, thoughtful, and considerate, we are showing respect. We might open a door for another person, smile, bring a chair over, and treat the person like he or she is a friend. We are able to see God's presence within the other person. As we treat others with respect, that same respect will be mirrored back to us.

Today I will think of ways to display my respect for God's creation. I will honor everyone I come into contact with today.

Dear God,

I wish to show respect for your creation. Please help me to treat everyone with the kind of respect I would wish for myself.

Thank you, God!

Ways I will honor others today: _____
_____
_____
_____

April 13
ACTING WITH DIGNITY

When a person acts with dignity, it means the person stays true to his or her principles, beliefs, and standards of behavior no matter what happens. The person is a model to others.

An example of acting with dignity means that if someone accuses you of something you did not do or calls you names, you do not respond by calling the other person names. Instead you stand by your truth. Ask God for strength and clarity in dealing with the situation. Ask that only truth be allowed to come forth. Then let it go.

Today I will act with truth and dignity.

Dear God,

Give me the strength to live my truth and model it to others. Help me to maintain high standards for my behavior.

Thank you, God!

How I can act with truth and dignity today:

_____
_____
_____
_____

April 14
QUESTIONING IS OK

Unless we question the what and why of things that happen, we may not fully understand what happened. The way we question is important. Questions or statements such as: "How did you feel when...." or "Help me understand what happened here" do not offend or make people feel threatened.

Your tone is also important. Do you sound accusing or angry? Getting to the truth is crucial to walking the path of truth. Everyone learns from it. It might be necessary to allow time to pass before you begin questioning. This allows time for your anger to lessen. For example, if you feel like shouting at a parent, you might want to take some time alone and then write your feelings on paper before discussing them calmly. Ask God to help you think it through lovingly.

Today I will question anything I do not understand. I will want to seek truth and understanding.

Dear God,

I wish to walk the path of truth and understanding. When I question, help me to use questions that seek truth but do not offend or accuse.

Thank you, God!

Situations I feel ready to question: _____

April 15

Today I stand witness to the many ways God works through me.

Thank you, God!

April 16
MONITORING TV AND ADVERTISING

Because you are in a stage of high growth, you are impressionable to messages and images portrayed on TV. Scenes or situations that show violence and inappropriate responses to anger may give you the idea that this is the way to act. An advertiser who uses wildly enthusiastic young people to sell sugary cereals or candy might influence you to eat something that is not good for you. They might give you the impression that everyone is doing it. Is this truth?

If you are unsure, ask your parents or someone you respect what they think about it. Read up on what the good foods are that you should eat. If you are informed, advertisers cannot fool you. Even adults can be fooled if they are not informed.

Lastly, choose TV programs that portray healthy family relationships and situations. If you are unsure about a program, ask your parents.

Today I will fill my world with positive images and messages. I will not be fooled by advertisers who just want to sell their products whether they are good for me or not.

Dear God,

Help me to see the truth about the images and messages I see on TV. Help me to question and gain understanding.

Thank you, God!

TV programs and movies I know my caregivers approve for me to watch: _____
_____
_____
_____

April 17

FEELING UNWORTHY OR FEAR OF SUCCESS

Many people sabotage their own success. They feel that they could not possibly be that good. Recently, a newspaper quoted a young man who scored extremely high on a national test in mathematics. His remark was, "It was nothing." If it was nothing, then why was his score higher than almost everyone else's? He probably had a hard time accepting the praise he was receiving or believing that he was that good. A better response would be "thank you."

Sometimes we read about athletes who cannot accept their success and who do something to stop their successes. They do not think they deserve that much success. They feel unworthy.

God wants us to be a success. If you find yourself having self-doubts, ask God to help you see your true worth in God's eyes.

Today I will look at myself in a mirror. I will tell myself that I am worthy to receive the good that God has coming to me and I am successful in anything I do when I partner with God.

Dear God,

Please help me to see my true worth. I wish to be a success in _____

_____

Help me to make it so.

Thank you, God!

April 18
ATTITUDE IS EVERYTHING

When you are faced with a task or problem, how you view it will determine the outcome. For example, if you have to raise some money for a bicycle or an event coming up soon, your thinking can determine whether you raise the money or not. These are some typical thoughts: "I can't do it!" "Maybe I can do it." or "I will raise the money for this concert and have money left for refreshments." Which statement do you think will produce the best results?

Think of what you want the outcome to be. Imagine it in your mind. Make a positive statement about what you are going to do. Then plan the steps required to get there. Your success will be ensured!

Today I will visualize what I want my results to be. Next I will make a positive statement about what I want to happen. Then I will thank God in advance for my success. Sit back and watch the miracles happen!

Dear God,

Miracles happen when I partner with you and keep a positive attitude. Please help me to be positive even when the going gets tough!

Thank you, God!

A result I want is: _____

_____

A positive statement about that result is: _____

_____

_____

April 19
ELIMINATING VIOLENCE

Violence can be eliminated when everyone finally believes that it is no longer an acceptable option. You can do your part to eliminate violence by refusing to watch TV programs or movies that promote violence. You can also pray daily for violence to be eliminated from our world. Most importantly, eliminate violence in yourself. In your mind, surround potentially violent situations with Divine Love and ask God to show you a better way.

If you have violence being directed at you, pray for God's highest good to be done. Ask adults to intervene if that is appropriate. Use peaceful words but also be firm. When God is working with you, miracles can happen.

Today I will eliminate violent thoughts and actions from my being. If I am feeling so angry that I am thinking violent thoughts, I will ask God to bring Divine Peace and show me a better way.

Dear God,

I pray that violence will be eliminated from every being on our planet. Show us the loving way to handle differences. Help me know how to model this new behavior.

Thank you, God!

Ways I can promote peace today: _____
_____
_____
_____

April 20
BLAMING YOURSELF OR OTHERS

Blaming is something you do when you are unable to accept responsibility for what happens. Perhaps you are playing a game in the house and a lamp is knocked over accidentally. Everyone points a finger at the person who knocked it over. In reality, everyone was involved in producing the situation.

Blaming does not help anyone. No one feels better with blaming, nor does it solve the problem. The best thing to do is to own up to your part and ask forgiveness. Think of ways you might remedy the situation.

Today I refuse to blame anyone for something I may have caused. I will accept my part and ask forgiveness.

Dear God,

Sometimes I have a hard time seeing my part in what happened. Make it clear, Lord, and give me guidance. Give me courage to own up and ask forgiveness.

Thank you, God!

Today I accept responsibility for my actions in the following incident:
_____
_____
_____
_____

April 21
BEING AWARE

Often we go through the motions but are not fully conscious of the people and events surrounding us. Being aware means slowing down enough to make every word, thought, or movement a conscious one. When you are conscious, you are more able to find joy in the moment or to change the outcome (if that is what you desire) before something unpleasant occurs.

This is particularly difficult when you are young because you are usually in a rush to experience everything and to grow up quickly so you can be an adult. That time will come soon enough. Cherish what you have now.

Today I will do everything consciously. I will live in the present moment.

Dear God,

Help me to be more aware of everything around me. Help me to find joy in the present moment.

Thank you, God!

The best parts about being the age I am: _____
_____
_____
_____

April 22
HONORING EARTH AND NATURE

God's beauty is in the nature we see around us every day. Take the time to smell the flowers, hug a tree, take a walk in the grass barefoot. Watch the sky and name the clouds and look again at night to see the moon and stars twinkling back at you.

Honoring the earth means to take care of it. Do not fill it with trash or just cut it down needlessly. Learn how to coexist with the animals. God called us to be caretakers. This means we have a responsibility to support the life growing in the air, land, or water.

Today I will take time to appreciate the nature God created for me. I will learn how to take good care of it.

Dear God,

Help me to see how I can be a good caretaker for the earth. Help me to always appreciate what you have given to us.

Thank you, God!

These are ways I can care for the earth today:
_____
_____
_____
_____
_____

April 23
FINDING MY WORTH IN MY COMMUNITY

Our community represents the family of God. We are a part of that community. What one person does to improve the community benefits everyone. For example, if you pick up trash in your neighborhood or visit someone who is ill, you are helping your community. When you plant flowers that everyone can enjoy, when you say prayers for the benefit of your community or participate in an event to raise money for a good cause that helps others, or when you mow the lawn and pull weeds for an elderly person on your street, it benefits your community.

No matter how young or old, everyone can do something to improve their community. What are some things you can do to help your community? Ask your parents if they have any ideas.

_____
_____
_____
_____

Today I will become more aware that I am a part of the family of God. What I do to improve my community will benefit everyone. Together we can make this world a better place.

Dear God,

I take many things for granted in my community...parks, transportation, services, cleanup. These things all help to improve my community so I can enjoy it more. Help me to see my part in all of this.

Thank you, God!

April 24

WINNERS AND LOSERS

Everyone's a winner! No one is a loser. We are playing games or sports for fun and to check our abilities against others. In the process it gives us more experience. Even if we lose, we win because we discover how we can do better the next time. We get more experience. There's no need to take ourselves so seriously that we put ourselves or others down about our playing. By encouraging the best in each other, we all win. Remember, it is only a game!

Today I will encourage myself and others to play our best.

Dear God,

I wish to play my best. Help me to do so in a way that brings out everyone's best.

Thank you, God!

What I have learned playing games or sports:

_____
_____
_____
_____
_____

April 25

Today
I choose to "Be."
I'm okay
just as
I am.

Thank you, God!

April 26
PERSEVERANCE

Being successful in life is at least in part due to perseverance. Perseverance is a quality that means that no matter how difficult things might get, you stick with it. Sometimes you might have an idea. It may not be the smartest idea ever thought of, but if you stay with it long enough, you will be successful.

Many times things look darkest just before a triumph. Don't quit! Persevere! Believe in yourself!

Today I will look at an area in which I will persevere. I will ask God for strength and courage to stay with it.

Dear God,

Sometimes I lose my interest in an area in which I should persevere. Teach me about perseverance. Give me your strength and courage and determination. With you as my partner, I will persevere!

Thank you, God!

Areas in which I ask God to help me "stick to it":

_____
_____
_____
_____

April 27
COURAGE

To have courage means that you are able to look at your fears and still charge ahead. There will be many times in your life when you will be asked to do something...perhaps make a speech in front of the class. You may be overwhelmed by fears of inadequacy. You think that you will faint on the spot! Everyone will laugh at you! Still you charge ahead.

Often later you find that your fears were unfounded. You were up to the task! Fears can become huge in our minds. They can immobilize us. Ask God to give you courage to overcome them. By using courage, you will grow and become more confident in yourself.

Today I will summon courage within me to overcome my fears. I will ask for God's help and inspiration.

Dear God,

I ask for courage. Help me to overcome my fears. Inspire me with your creativity and help me to grow in self-confidence and self-esteem.

Thank you, God!

I ask God to help me overcome these fears:

_____
_____
_____
_____

April 28
EXCELLENCE VERSUS PERFECTION

Striving for excellence is a worthy goal. Seeing yourself as perfect no matter what you do is the way God sees you. God holds us in perfection. We have only ourselves to convince.

Sometimes we get carried away with trying too hard to be perfect. If we worry too much about whether we can keep up with our ideals or if we find ourselves never quite matching up to our standards, then we have taken perfectionism too far.

By being the best we can be, we help ourselves to grow. If we get caught up in the perfection, we can stop our growth. God wants us to find joy in our lives. When the joy is not there, then we should reconsider what we are doing.

Today I will look at how I am living my life. I understand that I am not perfect and don't need to be perfect. I will strive for peace and joy in all I do.

Dear God,

Let me never lose sight of the joy and peace in my life. Help me to see the balance between being my best and trying to be perfect.

Thank you, God!

I might be trying to be too perfect when I: _____
_____
_____
_____
_____

April 29
HANDLING STRESS

Even young people have stress! Much is expected from them. Learning so many new ideas and disciplines can be stressful when you feel like playing and running outside with friends instead. Unhappy relationships in the home or having too many people to answer to also can be stressful.

Once in a while give yourself a break from the structure. Practice your music lesson at a different time. Do your homework on the bus or right after supper so you will have time for free play. Take a hot bath or watch a favorite TV show. Exercise!

Verbalizing your feelings can help you release the stress. Write your feelings in your diary or journal. Share them with parents if you feel comfortable doing so. Holding stress inside lowers your immune system and may result in illness. Stress interferes with your ability to concentrate and saps your energy. If you have been over-scheduled, talk to your parents about what you might be able to drop. Ask God for assistance in sorting it all out.

Today I will look at the stress I feel in my life. What can I do about it? Is it stress that I can handle or is it coming out negatively?

Dear God,

Help me to sort out my feelings. I want to know what alternatives might work to reduce the stress I am feeling.

Thank you, God!

Ways I can handle stress today are: _____
_____
_____

April 30
GROUP POWER

There is group power whenever people are gathered together. The energy of each person in the group is intermingled with that of the others. Soon everyone in the group begins to take on the same characteristics, wear the same type of clothes, think alike, and so on. This is why it is important to select carefully the group to which you belong.

Look at the members of your group. Are these the type of people you wish to be with long term? Did you choose them or did they choose you? Do they bring out the best in you or your worst? What do you have to give to each other? Sometimes you have to make the difficult decision to end a friendship.

Today I will take a close look at the group to which I belong.

Dear God,

Help me to choose good friends and to surround myself with positive influences. If I have not made good choices, help me in redirecting my life.

Thank you, God!

How my friends bring out the best in me:

_____
_____
_____

May 1

BUILD YOUR HOUSE ON A STRONG FOUNDATION: THE GOLDEN RULE

A life based on strong values will serve you well—honesty, integrity, kindness and concern for others, faith, and trust in God. Adopting the Golden Rule, "Do unto others as you would have them do to you" as a code for your behavior will also serve you well.

If you are dishonest, it will create problems in your life. Lack of integrity will affect your work and personal relationships. If you look closely at the people around you, you will see that any time they were not truthful with themselves and others, they paid for it. If you steal something from someone, you know there will be a consequence. When you are concerned about when the consequence will come, you lose peace of mind and possibly your freedom to move about as you please.

Today I will examine my life to make sure I am building a strong foundation of values for my life.

Dear God,

Guide me in building a strong foundation of values in my life. If I need to make adjustments, help me to do so. Bring the right teachers to assist me.

Thank you, God!

Values I cherish: _____
_____
_____
_____
_____

May 2
CREATIVITY: DECLARE IT GOOD

Through your thoughts, words, and actions, you are able to demonstrate your creativity. Perhaps you are writing a story or painting a picture. Maybe your talent is working with the earth or animals. Whatever you create, when you are satisfied with the results, thank God and declare it good.

That is what God did in creating earth and the heavens. On the sixth day, God looked at the creation and declared it good.

Not everyone will appreciate our creations. That is OK. Creations are as individual as the people who create them.

Today I will show my gratitude for the things that I create and I will declare them good.

Dear God,

Sometimes we take things for granted or are just unaware of what we are creating. Help me to find satisfaction in my creations. Then remind me to declare it good or to make the adjustments necessary!

Thank you, God!

Today I declare good in these things or situations I have created:

_____
_____
_____
_____

May 3
WHY AM I HERE?

We are here as Christ's ambassadors on earth to demonstrate God's love and forgiveness. This sounds very simple but it isn't. Have you ever had a fight with a friend and you did not speak to each other for a whole week? We can ask God to surround the situation in love and to give us a forgiving heart. Once we ask for God's help, miracles will happen. Hearts will soften and peaceful relations will be the end result.

All of us are learning and growing. We are demonstrating what we believe and who we think we are by our actions and words. This is constantly changing as we grow. There is nothing that God will not forgive if we have forgiveness in our hearts. We must forgive as God forgives. God's love is unconditional, which means God accepts us as we are...the good, the bad, and the ugly. God asks us to do the same with each other.

Today I will model love and forgiveness to myself and others.

Dear God,

Teach me about love and forgiveness. Help me to model it for others.

Thank you, God!

Ways I can model love and forgiveness:

_____
_____
_____
_____
_____

May 4

WE CAN MAKE CHOICES TO BE HEALTHY

When we do not hold a visual image of ourselves as perfect and well beings, we open the doorway to illness. When we make food choices that we know are not healthy for us, we also open the door to illness. There is another way illness enters. When we hold anger or grudges and do not forgive others, these feelings reside in our bodies and can make us sick. That is why it is very important to love and forgive.

Today I will picture myself as a whole and well being. I will ask God to surround me in Divine Love. If I have a hard feeling about someone, I will ask God to surround everyone involved and bring about forgiveness. I will choose love, peace, and joy in my life.

Dear God,

Help me to think of myself as whole and healthy...a perfect being. Give me a loving and forgiving heart. Surround me in your peace, love, and joy.

Thank you, God!

Ways to help God keep me healthy:
___
___
___
___
___

May 5
GIVING YOUR POWER AWAY

You are in the cafeteria line. A friend reaches over and grabs your dessert off your tray. "You don't mind if I have this, do you? You are such a good friend!" Your friend has used you by stroking your ego and taking something you wanted. If you do not speak up, you have just given your power away along with your dessert! This happens in many subtle ways.

When you give yourself no care or concern...when you put others ahead of you...or when you allow others to use you, you give your power away. Forgive yourself for doing this, and work to increase your personal power through better communications and courage. You need to be able to communicate what your needs are and to have the courage to speak up when you need to voice them.

Today I will observe my interactions with others.

Dear God,

Help me to develop my own personal power and not give it away, yet be mindful of the needs of others.

Thank you, God!

When am I giving my power away? _____
_____
_____
_____
_____

May 6

Today I forgive myself for any past wrong doings. This is the present. I choose to live guilt-free in the present.

Thank you, God!

May 7
FINDING THE JOY

No matter what we do in life, whether in work, recreation, or love, we need to find the joy. Finding the joy means to look for the good in everything and everyone. The power, imagination, creativity, intelligence, and energy will come from the joy found in your heart. This makes every moment an act of love.

Rather than doing for the sake of doing, you need to evaluate your life. Is what you are doing a reflection of what you wish to have in your life? Does it bring you joy? What do you wish you could do more of in your life? Then do it!

Today I will take a closer look at my life. Is what I am currently doing a reflection of my inner soul's desire?

Dear God,

Help me to be clearer about what I want to happen in my life. Then help me to make it so.

Thank you, God!

Today I will look for good in: _____
_____
_____
_____
_____
_____

May 8
FEAR

Fear is a paralyzer. It stops you from being your best. Perhaps you have a fear of trying a certain sport (such as skiing). What is your fear? Look at it. Do you fear for your safety? Or are you afraid others will laugh at you? Are you afraid you might not be successful?

If you do not really believe you will be hurt, then ask God for the courage to overcome your fear. Picture yourself surrounded by love. By overcoming your fear, you open the door to greater courage and more self-confidence. You open up to your own growth.

Today I will examine my fears and ask God's help in overcoming them.

Dear God,

Help me to examine my fears and know when they are stopping my growth instead of protecting me. Give me the courage to overcome fears which stop me from growing.

Thank you, God!

I can demonstrate God's ability to help me overcome this fear:
_____.
What I will do: _____
_____
_____
_____
_____

May 9
COMPETITION

Competition can help us to hone our mental and physical skills. Sports is one example in which everyone is given an equal chance. Competition between teams can help us to learn to work with others in a group for the group goal.

Competition can also make us feel separate and alone. Sometimes it can make us feel not good enough. When the emphasis is on winning rather than helping everyone to learn and be their personal and group best, then competition may not be as helpful.

Today I will ask God to help me keep my perspective about competition. I will show good sportsmanship to others.

Dear God,

I wish to do my personal and group best but not at others' expense. Help me to see myself as I really am when dealing with others.

Thank you, God!

What I can learn from competition: _____
_____
_____
_____
_____

May 10

HONORING MOTHERS

Mother's Day is an important day. It honors everyone's mother. Motherhood offers the opportunity for everyone to share unconditional love. No matter what a young person does, the child's mother still loves him or her. Mothers give unselfishly to their children all year long. They live a life of service and nurturing.

Mothers model for their children how they would like them to be as adults. They work to provide opportunities for growth for their children and to prepare them for the tough life of an adult. If you don't have a mother, is there a mother substitute you would like to honor?

Today I will honor my mother by letting her know I appreciate and am aware of her efforts. I will do something special, such as write a letter about those things I most appreciate, make something for her, or give of my time to do something she would like. I could also set aside time to spend just with her.

Dear God,

I thank you for my mother...the selfless time she has given to me, the love she has always offered to me, and the many things she has taught me. Help me to show my appreciation.

Thank you, God!

What I will do for my mother or another's mother today:

_____
_____
_____
_____

May 11
TELLING LIES

When someone tells a lie, it often requires another lie and still another, until the situation is impossible. Some people lie so often that they do not even recognize truth when they see it.

God is only truth. God encourages us to follow the truth. Jesus said "I am the way, the truth, and the life...." He was the walking example of how to live in truth.

You have a direct connection to God as God's child. If you are not sure whether something is truth or not, look within and pray to see the truth. What is that inner voice saying? It does not lie. If you feel lousy about something, it was not truth for you. This is one way God speaks to you.

Today I wish to experience only truth. If it is not truth, I do not want it in my life.

Dear God,

I want to experience your truth. Make it clear for me. If something is presented that is not truth, help me to release it from my life.

Thank you, God!

I can tell the truth when: _____
_____
_____
_____

May 12
RECOGNIZING OUR ONENESS

We are all One. We all need love, nurture, and acceptance. We need to be fed, to be clothed, and to have shelter from the elements. We are all children of God, connected in God's love.

Jesus said "Truly, I say to you, as you did it to one of the least of these my brethren, you did it to me." What that means is that the light of God is in all of us. When you help a fellow human who is in need, you are giving assistance to God, whose spark resides in that person.

Today I will help someone in need. I will pray for the highest good to come to my brothers and sisters in this world and to myself.

Dear God,

Help me to be aware of our Oneness. I wish to see your spirit shining forth in all I meet today. Allow your spark in me to be a testament to your love and compassion.

Thank you, God!

I will help God's children today by: _____
_____
_____
_____

May 13
HAVING A BAD DAY

Everyone has a bad day now and then. If we focus on the unpleasant things that are happening, then we can truly be brought down by it. Instead, say to yourself, "This happened, but I wish to be surrounded in God's love and energy. Help me to experience peace, joy, and a sense of humor." Then thank God for turning your day around.

Today I will laugh when something goes wrong. I will thank God for changing my attitude to one of peace and joy.

Dear God,

Develop in me an attitude of peace and joy. Let me see you in every person or situation I encounter today. Help me to see that having a bad day is a "choice" that I make.

Thank you, God!

My prayer for the next time I feel I'm having a bad day:
_____
_____
_____
_____
_____

May 14

LIFE'S EBB AND FLOW

Life has an ebb and flow. Sometimes things go very well for you, and other times it seems as if there is one obstacle after another.

The key is to keep your sense of humor. Be aware that things will turn around and be good again. Try to look long term rather than short term. This is difficult to do when you are young because you do not have the experience to realize that change will happen and things do get better. Look for the lesson you are to learn in what you are experiencing.

Today I wish to feel surrounded by God's love. When things go wrong, I will keep the faith that it will turn around and get better.

Dear God,

Help me to see clearly the lesson I need to learn. Develop in me faith, hope, and the ability to endure life's challenges.

Thank you, God!

A time when I noticed that things got better was:
_____
_____
_____
_____

May 15

PREPARING FOR SUMMER VACATION

Summer is a time when we look forward to the lazy pace. But, this also means that boredom can set in quickly if activities are not planned. Before summer vacation arrives, sit down with your family and brainstorm all the things you can do. Plan some quiet, rainy day items as well as outdoor activities. Post this list on the refrigerator or some handy place to refer to when you feel unimaginative.

If your family decides to go on a vacation, hold a family meeting. Let everyone say what they would like to see or do. Plan for some activities to keep you occupied during long car or plane rides. Obtain a map with the route outlined on it so you can follow along with where you are. Then you will not be asking so often, "Are we there yet?" Remember to give all family members space for their own thoughts. Being together on a long car ride can be trying if you do not respect each others' space. Do not forget kindness words such as "please," "thank you" and "excuse me."

Today I will make plans for my summer vacation and share them with my family.

Dear God,

Thank you for summer vacations. I am joyfully anticipating lazy days and summer activities. Even during this time, I will be learning life lessons. Help me to be a joy to those around me.

Thank you, God!

Some of my favorite rainy day activities are:
_____
_____

May 16

WHEN YOU FEEL SEPARATED FROM GOD

Sometimes we feel separated from God. Perhaps you have been very busy and have not given much thought to God. Or you may have chosen to do things you know are wrong and so you feel separated from God. Actually, God is always there. You may just not be aware of it. Pray that you will feel God's presence in your life.

Pray or take time to be in the quiet. Take a walk alone in the woods or just sit under a favorite tree. Maybe just sitting on your bike in quiet contemplation is enough. God takes you where you are. All that is required is your awareness and desire to be connected to God.

Today I will take time to talk to God.

Dear God,

I want to stay connected to you. I want to feel surrounded by your love. I know you are always there for me; help me to know your presence around me. Develop that awareness in me, God!

Thank you, God!

I will stay connected with God today by: _____
_____
_____
_____
_____

May 17
BEING FULLY THERE FOR OTHERS

Being fully there for another person means giving your undivided attention when talking to that person. It means giving of yourself without other distractions. For example, if you are watching television and trying to talk to a friend on the phone at the same time, you cannot give your friend your undivided attention.

Being fully there also means that you cannot witness another person's pain and not try to help. If there is some way you can help the person, you must do so.

Today I wish to be fully there for anyone I encounter this day.

Dear God,

Being fully there for another human being can be difficult for me. Help me to use my eyes, ears, and intuition in being with someone. Help me to see when I can be of assistance or offer empathy without trying to take over the person's problem.

Thank you, God!

Today these are the ways I will be a better listener:_____
_____
_____
_____
_____

May 18
FAILURE

Perhaps I didn't do so well in gym today or failed an exam. I can turn my failures into a good thing with God's help. I will ask myself, "What can I learn from failing on that test?" Do I need to study more about a certain topic? Do I need to have better study habits? Is there something I can practice to help me do better in gym?" Failures can always be turned into a positive by finding what we need to learn from them. If I dwell on the failure, I will only think poorly of myself.

Today I will look for what I can learn from my failures.

Dear God,

Help me always to look for the gift in my failures. Help me to treat myself with respect and compassion because I am your loving child. I will always to do my very best.

Thank you, God!

I can do better next time by: _____

_____

_____

_____

May 19
THE IMPORTANCE OF FRIENDS

Friends fill an important place in your life. They are there for your support and the sharing of growth experiences. True friends accept you as you are in good times and in bad.

Some friends are called acquaintances. Acquaintances are people you know and like but do not know very well and with whom you have not shared deep experiences. They cannot be counted on in times of crisis. A person with two or three close friends is indeed a fortunate person.

Today I will take a good look at my friends. Which ones can I count on in times of need? Those are the friendships I will develop and nourish.

Dear God,

Teach me to be there for my friends in their times of need as I hope they will be there for me. Show me who my true friends are. Thank you for the blessing of good friends.

Thank you, God!

Today I give thanks for these friends:

_____
_____
_____
_____

May 20

SUICIDE

Have you ever had thoughts about ending your life? Has a friend ever indicated they would like to end their life? If so, ask for help. Seek out someone who has survived life's tribulations and struggles, such as a minister or trusted adult, and ask him or her to help you regain your perspective. Young people have difficulty maintaining perspective sometimes because they do not have the experience of having survived struggles.

With every end, something new begins. You cannot expect to be good at everything. Find what you are good at and what brings you joy. Then work on that. Seek out a counselor or trusted adult to help you through your trial. Once you are stronger emotionally, you will be able to check out new options more confidently. Read an autobiography or biography about someone who has struggled and overcome difficulty, for example, Helen Keller or Franklin D. Roosevelt. See what that person learned from life experiences. Remember that life's struggles occur to teach us. We are not alone. Seek God's help. God will bring people to you who can help you. God will never give you a burden greater than you can handle. Struggles are God's way of refining and strengthening us.

Today I will turn my trials over to God's care.

Dear God,

Sometimes my burdens feel overwhelming. I just feel it would be easier if I were not here. I have hurt others and myself. I feel hurt and I feel ashamed. Please forgive me. Show me a better way. Make me a stronger person. Help me to learn from this.

Thank you, God!

Today I entrust God with these burdens:

_____
_____

May 21
PLAYING SPORTS

Being involved in sports is a great way to learn teamwork skills. It is also a good way to stay physically fit. Sports provides a means by which to develop close relationships with other people.

Through sharing common goals, victories, and failures we develop closeness.

Find a sport that you enjoy. It is not necessary to be involved in many sports at once. You can actually lose your focus and wear yourself down if you are involved in too many activities. Instead, once you have chosen a sport, give it your best attention and effort. Then stay with it so that you will be able to develop competence and self-confidence.

Today I will choose a sport I can enjoy while getting fit and developing friendships.

Dear God,

Help me to choose a sport and stay with it. Develop me into the best that I can be.

Thank you, God!

My favorite sport is _____
because _____
_____
_____

May 22
FEELING CONFUSED

Sometimes you may feel confused. Perhaps something has happened and you do not understand what you did or how you should view it. Another time you may feel confused about what you should believe in or stand for. You can ask God to clarify the situation for you.

Today I will ask God to help me see the truth in what happened and in my actions and thoughts.

Dear God,

I do not want to be confused. Surround me in your Divine Love and help me to see the situation clearly.

Thank you, God!

Right now I am confused about: _____
_____
_____

My thinking is clearest when I: _____
_____
_____
_____

May 23
BRING OUT THE BEST IN OTHERS

Jesus said, "You are the salt of the earth...." Just as seasoning brings out the best in food, you can bring out the best in others. How can you do this? Help others to see the better side of themselves.

Sometimes a friend has a low opinion of himself or herself or perhaps is surrounded by poor role models. Be a good role model for that person. Help your friend to think through consequences and discover more appropriate alternatives. Then be sure to acknowledge your friend when he or she makes good choices. Help the person to see himself or herself as a person of worth and contribution.

Today I will be a good role model for others and help them to see the best side of themselves.

Dear God,

Help me to bring out the best in everyone I encounter today. Help me to see your good shining through them.

Thank you, God!

I can best be a good role model today by:
_____
_____
_____

May 24

*Today
my heart is filled
with joy and awe
for the magnificence
of God's creation.*

Thank you, God!

May 25
HUMOR/LAUGHTER

Laughter is a balm for healing the soul. Research has proven that it has a positive contribution to the healing process. Laughter can ease tension and even diffuse conflict. Laughter is something that everyone can share because it points out the ironies of life.

Laughter should never be at another's expense. Jokes that put down another's sex or nationality are not appreciated by all. True humor is something that everyone can share equally. Topics that point out life's inconsistencies or common experiences are enjoyed by everyone.

Today I will cultivate my sense of humor. I will choose topics that offend no one. I will learn to laugh at myself.

Dear God,

Life can be so serious sometimes. When something happens to aggravate me, help me to see the humor in it. Help me to be discriminating in choosing humor that does not offend others.

Thank you, God!

The best joke I've ever heard that does not hurt anyone is:

_____
_____
_____
_____

May 26

DEALING WITH WALLS PEOPLE CONSTRUCT AROUND THEMSELVES

Do you know people who will only interact with people of a certain race, or who will only go to a certain church, or who wear only particular brands of clothes. When people will only interact with certain people, they construct imaginary walls around themselves to shut others away from them. Often in schools there are "cliques" that separate the academic students from the jocks or athletes; the creative, artistic types from the drugstore cowboys; and so on. What cliques have you seen in your school? Everyone wants to feel that they "belong." However, being a member of a group separates us from getting to know more about others. Instead, we see only the group's clothes or symbols.

The barriers that I see that I have created are: _____
_____
_____
_____

Dear God,

Help me to be open to all of your creation. Help me to be friendly and to look for the good in each person.

Thank you, God!

May 27
ANGELS

Angels are a gift from God. They watch over us. They love and guide us. They are there to help in times of need.

We can develop a personal relationship with our angels. First, we can thank God for sending them and thank them for being there watching over us. Second, we can ask God for their assistance in changing a bad habit. Ask them to join you when you pray.

Today I will give thanks for the angels God has sent to care for me.

Dear God,

Thanks for the angels who watch over me. Help me to be aware of all the ways they can help me. Show me ways to give appreciation.

Thank you, God!

Today I will ask God and my angels to help me work on:
_____
_____
_____
_____

May 28
HAPPINESS

What is happiness to you? For some people it may be the latest game or trinket. For others it includes things that cannot be bought, such as friends, peace within yourself, joy, a happy and supportive family, or doing well on a test.

Those things that can be bought are often fleeting. One minute we just have to own them. The next moment they are deep in the closet, completely ignored.

Relationships with family and friends last longer and have a greater benefit to us over the long run. Developing habits that allow you to consistently do well on tests also has long-term benefit. Learning to have peace within yourself has a lifetime benefit.

Today I will learn to appreciate and value those things that have long-term value for me.

Dear God,

Help me to learn the difference between what is good for me over the long term and those things that have fleeting value. Help me to make good choices.

Thank you, God!

True happiness to me is: _____
_____
_____
_____

May 29

HONORING PEOPLE WHO HAVE DIED FOR FREEDOM

Memorial Day is a day set aside to honor the people who gave their lives fighting in the armed services so that we can have freedom.

What is freedom? Freedom means we are free to do as we wish, to live where and how we please, to say out loud what we think without fear of being persecuted. We are able to follow the religious beliefs we desire. However, being free does not mean we may do anything we want without regard for the consequences.

Veterans have fought to ensure that our freedoms stay intact.

Today I honor those soldiers and civilians who have fought for our freedom. I will thank God for them.

Dear God,

Thank you for those soldiers and civilians willing to give their lives so that I could live as I wish today. Help me to live so that my life honors them. Give me the strength of will and conviction to fight for our freedoms and to promote peace. Help me to develop a sense of self-responsibility and accountability that freedoms require.

Thank you, God!

Freedoms for which I am grateful: _____
_____
_____
_____

May 30
HEALING YOURSELF

Research has proven that much illness is a result of emotional factors. When you are under stress or when you are angry, those emotions get stored in your body. Over time a lot of negative energy gets stored in your body and can come out in the form of illness.

When you are not feeling well, ask God to send healing light and love to surround you. Ask God to reveal to you if something you are doing is causing the illness, so that you might release it.

Writing down your thoughts and feelings is a good way to release them. Sometimes talking to a friend helps you to sort them out, too. Keep an attitude of love and forgiveness.

Today I will turn within to find out what I am holding onto that I need to release.

Dear God,

Develop in me an attitude of love and forgiveness. Reveal to me anything that I need to release. Send your healing light and love to surround me.

Thank you, God!

I release these emotions and their causes:

_____
_____
_____
_____

May 31
WIN-WIN STRATEGIES

A friend has asked you over to spend the night and go to a concert. You ask your mother for permission. She has a meeting and risks being late if she takes you. Your father is out of town. You are upset and feel defeated. What can you do?

A win-win strategy is when everyone gets something with which they can be happy. When conflict appears to arise, remember, you may have other choices. Could your friend pick you up? Could your friend meet you half way so that your mother won't be late? Is the concert available on another night that might work better for everyone? Look at all your alternatives. Of course, it helps if you do not do everything at the last minute. Plan ahead.

When someone walks away losing, he or she does not feel good. When both parties are able to get something, even if it is not exactly what they wanted, they still feel good about it. You will cultivate more friends and better relationships overall when you adopt the win-win approach.

Today I will think "win-win" on all situations I encounter.

Dear God,

Help me to be sensitive to everyone else's needs as well as my own. Help me to model a strategy that allows everyone to win.

Thank you, God!

One win-win approach I could take today is:
_____
_____

June 1

EVERYONE HAS A BAD DAY (BUT DON'T TAKE IT OUT ON OTHERS)

You forget your homework; someone forgets to put the key back after using it and you are locked out of the house; you forgot about a meeting you were to have attended after school and could not reach anyone to get a ride home. Now you won't be able to be in the class play.

These are examples of some of the things that can happen on bad days. They happen to everyone. When you begin to see a pattern, do not dwell on what a bad day you are having. Instead laugh! It will lighten things up.

Pray for strength and assistance to deal with everything and everyone who you come in contact with today. Ask for Divine Love to surround you and ease all situations that arise. Especially do not take it out on those around you. Admit that you are having a bad day. Everyone can relate to that and will either try to help you or keep away from you.

Today I will ask God to surround me with love. I will remind myself that I am Divinely Loved.

Dear God,

When the events of the day seem to conspire against me, help me to lighten up. Give me comfort and strength to deal with it.

Thank you, God!

Three ways I can lighten up are:
1. _____
2. _____
3. _____

June 2
HANDLING CONFLICT

When you are angry at a sibling or friend, it is hard to think straight. You may say words you do not mean. What could you do instead? First, allow a cooling off time for you and the person with whom you are angry to get your emotions under control. You may need to be separated from that person temporarily. Second, ask God to surround you both with love. Then you might try to think of ways you and your friend or sibling can meet both your needs. Use humor to ease tensions. Ask forgiveness if it is appropriate.

Remember that God asks us to use unconditional love. Even if we are not able to find a good solution for ourselves, God asks us to love the other person. Not doing so only hurts you.

Today I will live with the idea of forgiveness and unconditional love. I will experiment with different ways to deal with conflict.

Dear God,

Help me to deal with conflict lovingly. If I am unable to get my way, help me to release my anger constructively and forgive the other person.

Thank you, God!

Here is how I recently handled a conflict: _____
_____
_____

Here are some other choices I could have made in that situation:
_____
_____
_____

June 3

DOING CHARITABLE ACTS FROM YOUR HEART

Bringing joy to someone else through unselfish acts is the greatest way to bring joy to yourself. Do not do it to earn "Brownie Points"; do it because it brings you pleasure. God knows what is in your heart. Do not expect for your kindness to be returned. Sometimes it won't be. A kindness that you expect to be repaid is not a true gift. It would be as if you are taking it back.

When you feel God's love pouring through you, you will not care if anyone ever repays you. The more you do for others, the better you feel about yourself.

When it is not coming from the heart, stop doing it. If you feel like someone is taking advantage of your goodwill or that you are putting yourself in a state of exhaustion, stop! Only do those things that come from the heart.

Today I will examine my giving. What can I do to help others? How much time can I honestly give? Am I doing it from the heart?

Dear God,

I wish to serve others. Help me to organize my time and efforts so that I can serve others without over committing myself. Help me to know when I am serving from the heart.

Thank you, God!

Today I will do these things from my heart:_____
_____
_____

June 4
RESPECTING DIVERSITY

Maybe you have heard the phrase "Everyone's different but we're all the same." That's what diversity is about—young or old; black, red, white, or yellow; male or female; different nationalities, religions, and so on—God created us all! We all have the same emotions and needs...sometimes we have similar experiences; and we all have the same Creator!

Today I will look for all the ways in which I am similar to my brothers and sisters of the world. I will look at all cultures and races, sexes, and religions with new appreciation, knowing that we are all made in the image of our Creator. If I don't like someone's behavior or ideas, I will try to look for God's image in that person.

Dear God,

We are all the same and made in your image. Help me to have tolerance for every type of diversity, knowing that we are all part of the same family.

Thank you, God!

Talk to someone today who is of a different nationality or religion than you. What do you think you will find that the two of you have in common?

_____
_____
_____
_____

June 5

Today I live with hope and the promise of good things to come.

Thank you, God!

June 6
ACCEPTING MY GOOD

Sometimes people want to do a kindness or give us a gift. Maybe they give us a compliment. We reply "I don't believe that" or "You don't have to do that!" Actually, we often turn away good things coming to us by feeling that we are unworthy. We are worthy of great things! It is God's pleasure to give them to us.

To accept compliments, just thank the giver. To accept gifts, say "Thank you. How thoughtful! I am overwhelmed!" The giver gets to feel joy in your receiving. By not accepting gifts or compliments, you risk hurting the giver and turning off the flow of good coming your way.

Today I will become a good receiver as well as a giver of good.

Dear God,

Help me with the issue of worthiness. I know I am your beloved child. Help me to be gracious in giving as well as receiving good.

Thank you, God!

Turn to a friend and give him or her a compliment. Watch his or her reaction. Do you react that way? *Yes I always smile & say "thank you."*

June 7
LISTEN TO YOUR BODY

Your body can tell you what foods it needs if you will listen. It can tell you when you need to get more rest to fight off illness so that your body can cure itself. The trouble is that we do not always listen to it. In fact, old thinking of the past was to deny yourself and your body. Today some coaches will tell you to starve yourself for a swim meet or wrestling match. They will have you exercise to the point of over-fatigue or illness. Listen to your inner wisdom. What does it say? This is the only body you will have.

Today I will be still and listen to my body. It will tell me what I need to eat or do.

Dear God,

Develop in me an awareness of my body's needs. Help me to respect and take care of the wonderful gift that you gave me to experience life.

Thank you, God!

What good advice does my body give me? _____
_____
_____
_____
_____

June 8
LISTEN TO YOUR SELF-TALK

What is your self-talk? Listen to it. What are you telling yourself? Do you berate yourself and call yourself names or do you give encouraging messages. Are you limiting yourself with "I can't do this!" messages or are you saying, "I can do this and learn something in the process."?

Many people are very hard on themselves. They expect themselves to be perfect. In truth, they are in a learning mode and are not expected to do everything perfectly. Listen to your self-talk. Monitor it frequently. If you find that you are telling yourself something that is not true or is critical or judgmental, then say "Cancel, cancel!"[3] Ask God's help in restating what is really true. As you improve your self-talk, you will see everything around you improve also. Look into the mirror each day and affirm something positive about yourself.

Today I will monitor my self-talk. When I say something untrue or negative, I will ask God's help in restating what is truth.

Dear God,

Help me to see clearly what I am telling myself. It's OK for me to be kinder to myself. Help me to treat myself as if I were my own best friend.

Thank you, God!

Here is what I caught myself saying: _____
_____

Here is what I prefer to tell myself: _____
_____

June 9
FORGIVING YOURSELF

All of your life, you are growing and changing. There will be times when you make mistakes. You might even wish that you could shrink and hide somewhere. At these times, you will have to ask God to help you forgive yourself. If you find that you are replaying what happened over and over, you will need to ask God to help you break that thought pattern and bring love, joy, and peace back into your heart and mind.

Time will always help you to forget things that happen. Ask God what you were supposed to learn from the experience. God forgives you unconditionally, so why would you not forgive yourself?

Today I will keep my mistakes in perspective. I will keep a sense of humor about it, and when I cannot, I will ask God's help to see the gift in it.

Dear God,

Sometimes I am mortified by the mistakes I make. Please help me to forgive myself as you forgive me. Help me to learn from my mistakes.

Thank you, God!

What I've learned from my mistakes: _____
_____
_____
_____

June 10
FORGIVING PARENTS

Young people often feel that parents are on one side of the fence and they are on the other. Because parents hold the power to give privileges or take them away, young people feel threatened or resentful. They may second-guess parents on their decisions and feel that they could do a better job.

Actually, parents do what they are capable of doing at the moment and with the skills they learned from their parents. Parents have to teach skills and responsibilities that will turn young people into responsible and successful adults. Sometimes, this means that parents have to take a position that their teen does not like. This hurts the parents as much as the teen. But they do it because they love you and want the very best future for you.

Ask God to help you to forgive your parents for any hurts they caused during the process of raising you. Also ask God to help you understand what your parents are trying to teach you. Remember that once you leave your parents, you can no longer blame them for your actions. From that point on, your choices and consequences are your own.

Today I will try to understand what my parents want me to learn. If I am unsure, I will ask them. If I feel angry, I will ask God to help me understand my anger and let it go.

Dear God,

Sometimes my parents feel like my enemy. God, help me to feel the love that they are giving me and to learn quickly what they want me to learn.

Thank you, God!

I forgive my parents for: _____

_____

June 11
THE GRASS IS NOT ALWAYS GREENER

Many times when a situation is tough, we tend to look somewhere else and say, "If only I went to that school, I'd have more friends or life would be easier." The truth is that your problems are your own and will follow you wherever you go. You might move to the greatest place on earth, but you will still encounter the same problems. Look within to find the root of your concerns. Ask God to help you see clearly where you are thinking or acting in a way that does not benefit you.

Today I will not look elsewhere for the solutions to my problems. I will look within myself.

Dear God,

You know me better than I know myself. I am struggling with _____
_____
_____

Help me to see clearly where I might take steps to make it better.

Thank you, God!

June 12
ELIMINATING ADDICTIONS

Everyone has something they do compulsively. Maybe they bite their nails when nervous or excited. Perhaps they overeat on a favorite food or buy things just for the sake of buying. Usually, as a young person, these compulsive behaviors are minor, but as you get older, they can become serious, such as drinking, gambling, or smoking.

Learning to deal with your behaviors while you are young is important. Look at when you do it and what you are feeling when you do it. Does it make you feel happier or more secure? Is this truth? If your behavior is serious enough, you may need a mental health professional to help you. Otherwise you may need to write your feelings in a journal. Pray to God to see yourself as you really are and make the corrections you need to make. Write below the compulsive or negative behaviors you need to work on.

_____
_____
_____

Today I will ask God's help in making the corrections I need to make.

Dear God,

Please help me to see myself as I really am. Provide the inner strength I need to make these corrections in myself. Surround me with your love.

Thank you, God!

June 13
FOUL LANGUAGE

Young people are enticed to use foul language because they think it makes them feel more grown up or because they have seen teenagers or other adults use it. Swear words are inappropriate at any age if they offend another. They also do not add to communication except to add emphasis—depending on which word is used. Many swear words are just offensive.

Ask yourself, "Do I need to use these words to get my point across or can I use other, more acceptable words?" You are a model for others...even the friends you play with and younger brothers and sisters.

Today I will communicate with words that are not offensive to others. I will be a model citizen for others.

Dear God,

Sometimes I feel like swearing. When I do, I will ask myself if I will offend anyone around me or if my behavior will lead anyone else to model negative behaviors. Help me to see myself clearly and make the right choices. Let me never offend you with my words, God.

Thank you, God!

What are some things you can say instead of using foul language? For example, "Tough crunchies!"

___
___
___

June 14
BREATHE

Your body needs oxygen. Research was done on cells that were given plenty of oxygen. These cells were 200 years old when the lab where they were stored burned, and yet the cells were still alive! Imagine, 200 years! Given plenty of oxygen and the right nutrients, your body can serve you longer and give you a better quality of life. Exercise is a good way to get more oxygen into your body. Taking nice deep breaths help to calm you. Have you ever noticed that when you are stressed, you actually hold your breath? Observe others. Note that those people who are most uptight and unhappy are not breathing properly.

Here are a few methods to get more oxygen into your body:

- Go outside and run around your house several times.
- Imagine your belly as a balloon. Watch it expand as you inhale oxygen and then slowly let it out. Do this 10 to 12 times.
- Blow bubbles across a room, or imagine that you are.
- Do 20 to 25 jumping jacks swinging your arms high over your head.

The more oxygen you take in, the more energized you will feel. In addition, you will notice your mood getting better.

Today I will bring more oxygen into my life to improve both physical and emotional health.

Dear God,
Thank you for oxygen, the breath of life.

Thank you, God!

June 15
TEASING

Teasing is an action that often annoys the person being teased. Teasing can be a form of flirting and actually can be fun until we go too far. If it hurts the other person's feelings or makes the person angry or annoyed, then we know we have crossed the line between a good experience and a bad one. The teasing must stop and apologies be given to make amends. If teasing can be kept friendly and fun, it is acceptable.

Today I will not do anything that I would not want done to myself.

Dear God,

Sometimes when I am playing around with my friends or brothers and sisters, I get carried away. Help me to recognize when I am about to go too far. Help me to never do anything I do not want done to myself.

Thank you, God!

When I have been teased I felt:_____
_____
_____
_____
_____

June 16
FAITH

Jesus said, "For truly, I say to you, if you have faith as a grain of mustard seed, you will say to this mountain, 'Move from here to there,' and it will move; and nothing will be impossible to you." Jesus was talking about the faith you must have in God and in yourself because God acts through you. Believe that God will take care of you. Believe that God wants only good for you and is willing to help you solve your earthly problems if you ask. Believe in your own worth and ability to serve others.

Today I will believe in God and in myself and my abilities.

Dear God,

I want to develop in faith. Provide the opportunities that will help me to grow in faith.

Thank you, God!

My favorite story about faith is: _____
_____
_____
_____
_____
_____

June 17

**Today
I give thanks
for music.
It fills the silence
and lifts my spirit.

Thank you, God!**

June 18
EVERY DAY IS A NEW BEGINNING

Each day begins anew like a fresh page just turned in a book, waiting to find out how we will write it. No matter what has happened before, we are forgiven by our Creator and have a fresh chance to start again. How will you decide to live your day?

Today I will count my blessings and give thanks. I will live this day surrounded by God's love and joy. I will smile at everyone I meet and help those in need.

Dear God,

Thank you for new beginnings and a chance to start anew.

Thank you, God!

Today I will let go of the past and begin anew by:
_____
_____
_____
_____

June 19
OWNING A PET

Owning a pet is a joy and a responsibility. Pets give us love unconditionally. They teach us about life and caring for someone other than ourselves.

Often pets live in confined cages and are totally dependent on us for food, water, grooming, and a clean living environment. We must learn to be responsible in caring for the needs of our pets. This prepares us for a future time when we might be parents or caregivers ourselves.

Today I will thank God for the gift of my pet. I will take good care of it.

Dear God,

Help me to be a good caretaker for my pet. Thanks for the love my pet gives me.

Thank you, God!

The thing I like most about pets is: _____
_____
_____
_____

June 20
SUMMER SOLSTICE

Summer is a time when life is in full bloom. Everything is growing. The flowers are bright and colorful; the grass is green; the trees are bearing fruit. Everything is producing.

We are like summer. We spend many hours learning and finally are able to express our learning by drawing a beautiful picture, winning a competition, writing a report, or doing well on a test. Summer represents the good times...lots of sun and fun and everything is fertile and producing.

Today I will look at the fertile times in my life. I will give thanks.

Dear God,

Summer represents the full bloom of the seasons. I, too, will experience the full bloom of my life. Help me to always hear your direction so I will be able to receive all the good you have coming to me.

Thank you, God!

My plans for this summer are: _____
_____
_____
_____
_____

June 21
HONORING FATHERS

Fathers offer love and nurture. They model the masculine side...offering a more logical, concrete view of the world, strength, knowledge, and special skill sets. Fathers mentor their children and often are able to develop fun-loving relationships with them. Fathers work tirelessly behind the scenes providing security and stability in the home. If you do not have a father who is with you now, is there a male "father substitute" in your life? You can choose to honor him.

Today I will reflect on what my father or father substitute has given to me. I will do something special to honor him by writing a letter of appreciation, giving my time to do something for him, or spending time with him.

Dear God,

I give thanks for my father...the selfless time he has given me, the nurture he has given me, and the love he has held for me.

Thank you, God!

This is what I will do for my father or someone else's father to say "Thanks!" _____
_____
_____
_____

June 22

BRIGHTEN THE CORNER WHERE YOU ARE

To brighten the corner where you are, you need only to smile and let your light shine forth. Tell a joke; plant some flowers; organize a group of friends to pick up a trashed area; put up a poster that will inspire others. These are all different ways to brighten your corner. Can you write down a few?

1. _____
2. _____
3. _____
4. _____
5. _____
6. _____

Today I will brighten the corner where I live. I will let my light shine brightly.

Dear God,

Inspire me to think of different ways to brighten the corner where I live. Help me to realize that I can do this without spending money—using only energy and thought.

Thank you, God!

June 23
ACCEPTING CONSTRUCTIVE CRITICISM

Sometimes we are not able to see ourselves as others do. We think we know ourselves, but we are not always on the mark. If someone criticizes you, you need to ask yourself, "Is there any truth in this?" If you are unsure, you might ask some friends who know you well if they agree with what was said.

Next ask God to help you see yourself as you truly are so that you can make the changes that need to be made.

Today I will ask God to help me see myself in truth and to make the changes I need to make.

Dear God,

Criticism is hard to take. Help me be open to those changes I need to make.

Thank you, God!

Changes I need to make: _____
_____
_____
_____
_____

June 24
ACCEPTING CONSEQUENCES

Sometimes consequences that seem harsh and hard to accept happen when we make bad choices. When this occurs, ask God to help you learn the lesson you need to learn and to accept the consequences of your choices. Ask God to help you make better choices next time and to think of the consequences in advance before the choices are made, so that you have a chance to change them.

All of us have a part of us that is hidden from ourselves. Shining a light on that part is painful, but it is necessary for self-improvement.

Today I will think of all the alternatives and possible consequences before I make any choices.

Dear God,

You see all things. Help me to see the consequences of my actions and choices before I make them. Help me to make good choices.

Thank you, God!

Good choices today include: _____
_____
_____
_____
_____

June 25
BE HAPPY!

Being happy is a choice. It is also a state of mind or being. No one can make you happy if you do not want to be. Nor can any "thing" make you happy. Many people go in search for happiness only to find it was within them all along. Have you ever thought a special sweater or game would make you happy, only to find that it no longer held the charm once you owned it?

Wake up each day and say to yourself and God, "Today I will be happy." Then make it so.

Today I will choose to be happy.

Dear God,

I give thanks to you for the chance to be happy. I know I make this choice. Help me to model to others the many ways I can show being happy.

Thank you, God!

I am happy today because: _____
_____
_____
_____

June 26
PRAYING

To pray, you need only to talk to God in your own words. Tell God what you are feeling or any concerns and what your intentions are.

Pray for the good of others and for your world. Pray that everyone will be uplifted in consciousness and for the release of all addictions. Pray to see yourself and others in truth. Tell God of your gratitude for all the blessings you have received. Ask for increased awareness of all that God has to offer.

Pray for your loved ones and yourself, that you are able to grow to your highest potential and receive all the good God has coming to you. Pray to release all negative emotions and feelings. Give thanks and acknowledgment to God for the positive outcome of your prayers.

Today I will pray from my heart for myself and others, knowing that all prayer is acceptable to God.

Dear God,

Help me to know when you hear my prayers. Help me to express what my heart is feeling in prayer.

Thank you, God!

Today I pray for: _____
_____
_____
_____

June 27

*Today I give thanks
for my family, friends,
and acquaintances who
fill my life with joy and love.*

Thank you, God!

June 28
NEW IS NOT ALWAYS BETTER

You may see advertisements that claim a product is new, or improved, or better than before. However, new is not necessarily better. Is the item able to function better now than it did before? Does the advertisement mean it will replace something that works...just maybe not as fast or good? Then what happens to the old item? Can someone else use it or will it be another item for the garbage? Where will the garbage go? How will it affect the earth? Other considerations might include: Are there more chemicals in the new product? Is there any hazardous ingredient? Is there anything that might cause allergies? How will it be disposed of at the end of its life? Is it biodegradable?

As you can see, everything has an impact on our world and us. Give careful consideration to each item you buy. Do you need it? Will it perform a specific function in your life or are you giving in to an impulsive moment. Think!

Today I will make wise decisions concerning my purchases. I will be a good caretaker of the earth.

Dear God,

Help me to make good decisions regarding the things I need. Teach me to take good care of the earth.

Thank you, God!

Purchases I am considering: a camera phone

June 29
BEING CRITICAL OR JUDGMENTAL

When you are critical or judgmental, it means that you are viewing others through eyes that reflect the rules, standards, and values that you have adopted for yourself. These may have developed as a result of your parent's training, unwritten rules of the society in which you live, your religious beliefs, your experiences, and so on. They may have nothing to do with the beliefs and experiences of the person whom you are judging. Each person operates on his or her own belief systems.

We are all on a spiritual journey, and it does no good to judge others. We can be discriminating in those people with whom we wish to spend time. For example, usually we want our friends to have similar belief systems. However, judging others will only cause others to judge us. We may not wish to operate under their belief system.

Truly, we need only to support and encourage each other in our growth and connection to God.

Today I will respect others for who they are. I will make no judgments about them.

Dear God,
I wish to pray for the highest good and potential to come to everyone. Help us to support each other in our growth.

Thank you, God!

What I hope others will see in me: _____
_____
_____

June 30

THE BALANCE BETWEEN SPIRIT, MIND, AND BODY

In order for our life to have balance, we need to nurture our body, mind, and spirit. This means that we need to feed our body well, exercise it, and give it medical care when necessary. We need to exercise our mind by developing our mental capabilities such as problem-solving, critical thinking, and creativity.

Our spirit needs nurture in learning to understand and manage feelings and emotions; how to connect to our higher power, God; learning to express our inner creative energy; ridding ourselves of addiction and negative behaviors; learning unconditional love and forgiveness; and uncovering and expressing our life's purpose. Our life's purpose is the reason for which we were created. It is our contribution to the world in which we live. All of this is a lifelong process.

Today I will ask God's guidance in helping me balance body, mind, and spirit. I will exercise my body. I will limit the amount of TV I watch and concentrate on doing a good job on my homework. I will ask my parents to help me plan two ways to nourish my spirit.

Dear God,

Help me to be consistent in taking care of my body, mind, and spirit so that I can maintain my balance. Help me to know when I get out of balance so I can make corrections.

Thank you, God!

Ways to nourish my spirit: _____
_____
_____
_____

July 1
BEING A GOOD WINNER

A good winner is a person who takes pride in his or her team's effort but does not flaunt it. A good winner acknowledges that everyone had a part in winning and brings out the best effort in the other members of the team.

A winner maintains a good attitude even in the face of adversity. And a good winner does not revel in the glory for too long, knowing it is only a small moment in time. There will be many more opportunities to excel in the future.

Today I will be a good winner and will work to see that all team members have their moment of glory.

Dear God,

Sometimes I get caught up in how good I am playing and forget there are others on the team. Help me to always be a good team player and winner. Help me to give credit to others as well.

Thank you, God!

A team member or classmate who deserves recognition is:
_____
For: _____
_____

July 2
BEING A GOOD LOSER

Being a good loser can be tough, especially when you put forth your best effort and the score is close. There are usually many thoughts of "If only...." or "I wish I had...." Being a good loser is important. On another day you will have another chance to win. Losing a game is not life or death! There should never be name calling or rude remarks.

Be proud in your effort and do not make excuses. Look for what you can learn from those who won. Shake hands with your opponents and say, "Good game!"

Today I will be a good loser if necessary and treat my opponents with the respect they deserve. I will look for what I can learn from them.

Dear God,

It is hard to be a loser sometimes. If I played my best, it is all I can ask of myself. Help me to see where I can improve. Help me to not take myself too seriously.

Thank you, God!

Areas in which I can improve: _____
_____
_____
_____

July 3
HANDLING ANGER

Everyone gets angry at times. How you are able to handle your anger is the key. Once you identify why you are angry, you can ask God for ways to release it. Allow time for you to get your anger under control. People often need a physical release. You might choose to ride your bike, run, scream out loud, or punch a pillow. It is okay to be angry. It is not okay to call names, hit, kick, or physically fight. Set a time when you can get back together and discuss things calmly. Ask someone who has no reason to take sides to act as a mediator if necessary. Try to work for a win-win situation. (See page 151.)

Today I will work on handling my anger positively.

Dear God,

Help me to get calm and see the problem clearly. When I am angry with someone, surround both of us in your love. Help us to release our anger and come up with a suitable compromise.

Thank you, God!

Options I have to release anger without hurting anyone:

_____
_____
_____
_____

July 4
CELEBRATING THE 4TH OF JULY

The 4th of July marks the birthday of our nation. It marks the first time that men and women of different cultures, nationalities, and religions were able to come together and permit the type of governance that allowed all to lead their life in the way they chose. Unlike some other countries, where a citizen voicing an opinion on government might be imprisoned, Americans are allowed and encouraged to voice their views. Men and women hold equal voting rights, too. In such a diverse culture it is key that individuals learn to respect each other's viewpoint even if they do not agree.

Americans have also been allowed to choose their lifestyle and occupation. This has permitted anyone with the desire to attain wealth to do so through their own efforts and not because of social status or barriers. Americans volunteer their time in service to others more than most nations around the world.

On our dollar bill is the national motto, "In God We Trust." Americans have always been a people of faith in God regardless of how an individual chose to practice that faith.

Today I will take time to appreciate all of the freedoms that we have available to us in this country.

Dear God,

Thank you for the United States. Thank you for our freedoms, diversity, and ability to rise above our status if we so choose. Please bless all our leaders with wisdom and compassion. Bless all of the people in our country with love, peace, and a grateful heart.

Thank you, God!

Freedoms I appreciate: _____
_____

July 5
NEVER SAY "NEVER"

There are many times when we are young that we are tempted to say "I will never do that!" Later, we have to eat our words. Issues become more clear as we get older, and then things we never thought we would do, we do. Perhaps we develop more courage or have more faith in ourselves. Or perhaps our beliefs have changed.

It might be better to say, "I do not think I'll ever do that, but time will tell."

Today I will use statements that are not so absolutely firm. I will leave room for my own evolvement and change.

Dear God,

Life seems so simple and black and white to me. I know that often issues are more complex than they appear. Help me to be flexible in my words so there is room for growth.

Thank you, God!

Ways I can be more flexible and leave room for change in the future:
_____
_____
_____
_____

July 6
SMILES AND GREETINGS

Smiles are a gift that can brighten your day. Have you ever noticed that sometimes if you are having a bad day and someone smiles at you or says something kind, it brightens your whole day? Maybe someone lets you ahead of her in the cafeteria line or shares part of her lunch because you forgot yours. Another student helps you with homework you could not understand. It is the small kindnesses we receive in life that make our days much brighter.

Today I will smile frequently and acknowledge others by saying something nice about them. I will look for a chance to do an unexpected kindness and witness the results.

Dear God,

Help me to give and receive small kindnesses. Help me to smile frequently to brighten others' days. Thank you for these small gifts that brighten my days.

Thank you, God!

Times when my day has been brightened by another:
_____
_____
_____
_____

Times when I have brightened someone else's day:
_____
_____
_____
_____

July 7
DISCRIMINATION

Discrimination happens when you make a distinction in favor of or against a person or thing. You can be discriminating about what behaviors or beliefs you are willing to accept, but when you discriminate against a race, religion, or sex, then you are not realizing that we are all one—created by God.

We are called upon to have respect for all living things because God created them. We do not have to believe as they believe or act as they act, but we do need to help them in their growth as we are helped in ours. Their basic needs must be met.

We can be a good role model of our beliefs. If we do not believe as someone else believes, we can still respect each others' differences.

Today I will show respect for all of God's creation and give thanks for our differences.

Dear God,

Help me to be tolerant of others. Variety is the spice of life. I know there are many ways to live. I wish to be open to learning about all of our differences.

Thank you, God!

Some differences I respect are: _____
_____
_____
_____
_____

July 8
POINTING OUT MISTAKES

You may not wish to point out others' mistakes if you do not want them to point out yours. At school or at home it is often tempting to call attention to something that someone did or something a person should have done but did not. Actually, we notice because we have probably done it ourselves. If you really wish to be helpful, you might say something directly to the person who needs to correct the situation. You might add, "I'm mentioning this because I've done it too." That way the person will feel more comfortable about it. You might even relate one of your own "dumb mistakes." Laughing at yourself is even better.

God wants us all to learn. Often when you are sharing something that happened to you, you find that everyone else has experienced something similar. Knowing that God is directing our learning in the classroom or out, we can be more tolerant of ourselves and others and assist each other.

Today I will help myself and others as we learn our lessons.

Dear God,

I wish to be cooperative in helping myself and others in learning our lessons. Make me aware if I do something that points out another person's errors.

Thank you, God!

Mistakes I have made that I am willing to tell to others:
_____
_____
_____
_____

July 9
APPRECIATING MYSELF

You appreciate yourself when you can see your good qualities. Look at yourself in the mirror now. Tell yourself, "I love you." "I trust you." "You are worthy of receiving good things."

Then describe why you like yourself. Include your good qualities. Write them down. Think about it during the day and add to it. Ask others what they like best about you.

Today I am learning to appreciate myself.

Dear God,

I am taking time to appreciate myself. Help me to see myself as you see me.

Thank you, God!

I like myself because: _____
_____
_____
_____
_____

July 10
MODELING JESUS' LIFE

What is Jesus like? Jesus has such faith in his relationship with God that he gave up all his worldly possessions, knowing that God would take care of his needs. He demonstrated that through our relationship with God, we could grow in faith and be in tune with God...that we could rise out of our self-centeredness and negativity to live a life of spirit and serving each other.

Jesus modeled unconditional love and forgiveness—even forgiving those who crucified him. He calls us to love and honor everyone without exception, forgive everyone without exception, and serve others. He also calls us to develop our faith to the point that we do not have doubts. This is what Jesus is about. He is our role model.

Today I will grow to be more like Jesus.

Dear God,

When I come across a struggle in my life, remind me to ask myself, "What would Jesus do?" Help me to be the best that I can be in your eyes.

Thank you, God!

Concerns I have today: What would Jesus do?
_____   _____
_____   _____
_____   _____
_____   _____

July 11
FINDING BALANCE

In the spaces below, write down all the activities you do during a day. Then next to them write "B" for body if it helps your physical body; "S" for spirit if it helps you develop spiritually; or "M" for mind if it helps you develop your mind. Then tally up each category. Where are you out of balance? Do you need to take some activities out of one category and add some in others? There will be times when you are out of balance for a while, but it should not continue indefinitely. Check your progress every quarter.

Sometimes we take better care of others than we do of ourselves. Handling this correctly is part of finding the balance.

Today I am working to create balance in my life.

Dear God,

Help me to see when my life is out of balance and needs correction. I have faith that whatever you prepare for me will be for my good.

Thank you, God!

Activities   Body/Spirit/Mind

_____   _____
_____   _____
_____   _____
_____   _____
_____   _____

July 12
BE ALIVE!

God has given us the great gift of life. Rejoice in it! Experience it in as many ways as possible. Some people put so many rules, fears, and restrictions on themselves that they are only able to live life through others. If this is you, break out of the shell. Try something bold, daring, and new. Do not just follow paths others have made, make one for others to follow!

Be alive!

Today I will embrace life by trying something I was afraid to do or doing something that is out of character for me but is still in line with God's will.

Dear God,

I wish to experience all you have to offer. I thank you for the gift of my life. Increase my awareness of all the many ways I can embrace life.

Thank you, God!

Something new I will try is: _____
_____
_____
_____
_____

July 13
GROWING THINGS

Watching a plant grow once you have nurtured it can bring great satisfaction. Just like us, the plant grows, seeds itself, blooms, and eventually declines. The plant is able to live on through seedlings or offshoots. It can be strengthened by pruning, just as we are strengthened by removing bad habits or addictions.

Plants are often able to survive harsh conditions of under watering, over watering, improper nutrients, or inappropriate amounts of sun. We too survive under less than perfect conditions only to emerge stronger in the long run. We too have to pay attention to what our body, mind, and spirit require to sustain us. If you are a person who often kills plants, perhaps you need to ask yourself, "Am I taking good enough care of myself, or do I ignore my needs as I ignore the plants' needs?"

We all were formed by the same Creator and experience our oneness even with plants.

Today I will nurture a plant and observe what it might be telling me.

Dear God,

I wish to flourish like my plant. Help me to take good care of myself. Help me to see what I can learn from plants and the earth.

Thank you, God!

What I can learn from plants is: _____
_____
_____
_____

July 14
SHOWING REVERENCE FOR LIFE

God created all living things...insects, birds, deer, cats, and all living creatures. He placed humans on earth to be caretakers over the earth and its creatures. Sometimes people do not realize the preciousness of life. God's spirit is in each creature. God's love flows through its being. Stomping on caterpillars or terrorizing dogs, cats, or any other living creatures is not acceptable to God. Hunting is permissible when the meat is used to feed someone, but killing for the sake of killing is not. Show your love of your Creator by taking care of God's creation.

Today I will treat every living creature with the love and respect I would show God.

Dear God,

Teach me how to be a good caretaker of your creation. Allow your love to flow through me to all your living creations.

Thank you, God!

Creations I can care for today are: _____
_____
_____
_____
_____

July 15
TRASHING THE EARTH

Some people believe that by throwing their trash on the ground they are providing jobs for others. This is an erroneous thought. Other people are just unconscious when they do it. They do not realize that their trash is an eyesore for others and that it is unhealthy for earth.

Some trash is not biodegradable. This means it will not break down and return to dirt. An apple core will break down, but a plastic cup will not. Animals may feed off an apple core, but a Styrofoam cup could cause digestive problems for animals. Have you ever seen a duck whose neck is being strangled by plastic rings pulled off pop cans? Animals can be endangered by our trash.

Today I will dispose of trash responsibly and recycle what I can so that I can appreciate the beauty of God's earth and protect the animals.

Dear God,

You have given us such a beautiful earth. Help us to show our appreciation and to be responsible with our trash. Show us a better way to handle trash.

Thank you, God!

Today I will help dispose of trash properly by: _____
_____
_____
_____

July 16
BEING ACCOUNTABLE

Being accountable means that people can count on you to complete a task. When it is your responsibility, you alone take credit if it is late, on time, broken, well done, and so forth. You are fully accountable for the completion of the task and the quality of the product.

One way you are accountable today is for your homework. You alone are responsible if it is done or not, turned in or not, correct or not.

We are all accountable for our actions and reactions. No one else has control of them but us. If you act or react inappropriately, only you can take credit or blame. What other ways are you accountable? List several things for which you are accountable.

1. _____
2. _____
3. _____
4. _____

Today I realize that I am accountable for my actions, reactions, and responsibilities.

Dear God,

Being accountable is scary. I know you are preparing me in small steps so I can grow into being more accountable.

Thank you, God!

July 17
SINGING SONGS

Singing songs is a way of expressing our inner soul and feelings. Although some songs have no real meaning, others have lyrics that express deep thoughts. Singing is joyful, sometimes thoughtful. Songs can bring us to tears or make us get up and dance. The rhythms move us. During the process of singing, we are bringing more oxygen into our system. This makes us feel better. It is hard to be sad when you are singing.

Many songs are sung to God and about God...perhaps because singing is such an expression of the soul. Be sure the words of yours songs are acceptable to God. Don't be concerned about whether you have a good voice; just be joyful!

Today I will sing my heart out.

Dear God,

Thank you for the gift of music and singing. Help me to express my inner feelings through singing.

Thank you, God!

My favorite songs to sing are:
_____
_____
_____

July 18
TELLING STORIES

In times past and in some cultures today that have not developed a written form of their language, the history of the people was passed from one generation to another through a Story Teller. This is how people learned from each other about life and the past. Today there is a revival happening in story telling. Because of the advancement of technology, our lives are changing drastically from generation to generation. It is important to share the knowledge of what transformations occurred and how they affected people's lives. Ask your grandparents or other older adults what it was like growing up in their time. Do an interview with them. Write a short biography about them. Here are some questions you might ask:

1. What was life like when you were young?
2. What was school like?
3. What invention most changed your life?
4. What decisions or choices would you have made differently?
5. What did you like best about that time?
6. What do you like best about this time?
7. What were your greatest successes and failures?

Now add your own questions and record the answers.

Today I will ask questions about the past so I can learn from it.

Dear God,

Telling stories is one way we pass knowledge from one generation to another. Help me to ask the right questions to learn what you would like me to learn. Help me to appreciate those who have come before me.

Thank you, God!

People I will interview: _____

July 19
YOU CAN'T PLEASE EVERYONE

You cannot please everyone. To try is to set yourself up for failure. Is what you are doing or thinking pleasing you? Is it hurting anyone else? Is it hurting you? Would God approve? If you are not hurting yourself or anyone else and if God would approve, then you have nothing to worry about. If you are not sure whether God would approve, then ask God to see the answer clearly.

To live your life pleasing others is to not realize your own true potential and gifts. God asks you to be of service to others but not to be subordinate or less than others.

Today I accept that I cannot please everyone. I will honor others even when I cannot please them.

Dear God,

Sometimes I feel bad about myself when others are displeased with me. Help me to see when it is impossible to please others and to accept it without feeling bad about myself.

Thank you, God!

I do these things that please both me and God:
_____
_____
_____

July 20
LOSING A PET

Losing a pet is a painful experience. Realize that your pet will always be with you in spirit.

To help you get through the pain of grieving, celebrate the joy of what your pet gave to you. Draw a picture of your pet; conduct a funeral service. Make up a song about your pet, or do a collage of pictures you took of your animal friend. Realize that even though your pet is gone, the memory lives on through your thoughts and in your heart.

Today I will focus on the joy of having had my pet. I will ask God to comfort me in my grief.

Dear God,

Thank your for _____ (pet's name). I give thanks for the joy my pet brought to my life. Comfort me in the loss of my friend.

Thank you, God!

July 21
FIRST IMPRESSIONS

People often accept or reject others based on their first impression. What impression do you make? Do you have good grooming habits that show you care about yourself? Do you exude confidence in yourself and your abilities? Do you respect others? How do you handle yourself in social situations? Do you offer your hand to shake or a ready smile? Do you acknowledge the other person or are you so absorbed in yourself that you are unable to reach out to the other person?

A spiritual person will try to look deeper than on the surface. A spiritual person will try to get to know the inner part of the other person. However, initial impressions tell others a lot about you. Look at yourself in a mirror right now. If you were meeting yourself for the first time, describe what you would see. Record it here:

_____
_____
_____
_____

Today I will be more aware of the impression I make on others. I will make an effort to reach out to others and get to know their inner spirit.

Dear God,

I know beauty is only skin deep. Help me to develop my inner beauty. Also help me to see more deeply into the spirit of others. May your light shine through me to everyone I meet today.

Thank you, God!

July 22
GIVING ADVICE

When a friend discusses with you a problem he or she is having, usually the person is asking for someone to just listen. Advice is only worth what you pay for it. The answers to you or your friend's challenges are within each of you. As your friend is describing the situation, ask questions that help to clarify or ask your friend to make choices. Avoid giving advice. If your advice fails, your friend may blame you. If it succeeds, you may be tempted to say "I told you so!" This will not further your relationship. The best thing to do when a friend wants to discuss a problem is to say, "I am willing to be a sounding board so you can think about your alternatives out loud and make choices, but I do not give advice."

Today I will be a sounding board for my friends when they need it, but I will not interfere in their problem-solving by giving advice.

Dear God,

Help me to be a good sounding board and to know when I am getting too involved in the drama of other people's lives.

Thank you, God!

People for whom I can be a good sounding board:
_____
_____
_____
_____

July 23
RANDOM ACTS OF KINDNESS

Showing kindness when it is unexpected can have a profound effect on others. They will be likely to pass it on to someone else, and those people will pass it on to someone else, and so on. This kindness might include a smile, allowing someone to cut in line ahead of you, befriending someone who frequently feels left out, or giving someone a flower or card to show your appreciation. These kindnesses cost nothing and often have a ripple effect. It is one way of letting your light shine.

List some things you could do today as random acts of kindness:
_____
_____
_____
_____

Today I will do an unexpected kindness for _____
_____.

Dear God,

Thank you for the joy I feel when I bring your light to others. Give me some ideas for ways to do kindnesses for others.

Thank you, God!

July 24

*Today
I am in tune
with the Oneness
of all God's Creation...
We were created
in love and in love
we will return.

Thank you, God!*

July 25
FEELING SORRY FOR YOURSELF

Now and then an event does not go as you had planned. Perhaps someone gets sick and an event cancels, or someone promises to take you somewhere and then does not follow through. You are disappointed. Then you start to feel sorry for yourself. When you see this happening, acknowledge it. Then forgive the person or persons who caused this disappointment. Ask God to help you let it go. Then ask to be brought back to inner peace and joy.

Today I will let go of disappointments and feeling sorry for myself. I can control how I feel, and I choose to feel joy and peace.

Dear God,

When I begin to feel sorry for myself, help me to turn it around. Help me to forgive anyone who was involved and to surround them in love. Once I let go, I will be free to experience peace and joy again.

Thank you, God!

I let go of these disappointments: _____
_____
_____
_____
_____

July 26
WHINING AND COMPLAINING

By whining and complaining, we focus more energy and attention on what is bothering us. We become part of the problem rather than part of the solution. Whining and complaining are activities that are not uplifting for us or for others. Ask yourself instead, "What can I do about this situation?" If you have no control over it, then ask God to help you to accept it. If you can change it, ask God to help you see the best solution and act on it.

Today I will let go of whining and complaining.

Dear God,

Help me to see when I am engaging in whining and complaining. Show me instead how I can change the situation or how to accept it if I cannot. Let my actions always uplift both me and others.

Thank you, God!

Situations I am turning over to God, releasing into his care:

_____
_____
_____
_____

July 27
I CAN'T CHANGE

Sometimes we hear someone say, "I can't change; this is the way I am." Think back to last year. What have you learned since last year? In truth, we are always in the process of change. The illusion is that we are not changing. In our effort to feel more secure, we want everything to stay the same.

God can help us to make the difficult changes we cannot make for ourselves. Tell God what you need to change and put it into God's care. Then let go of it. Do not try to work on too many things at once.

Today I will ask God to help me in making this change:

_____
_____
_____

I place it in God's loving care.

Dear God,

Change is hard for me. Grow my faith so that I will feel your protection and security no matter what changes are taking place. I know that you are directing my life.

Thank you, God!

July 28
LEARNING FROM THE PROCESS

When you are playing in the game of life, it is not so important what the outcome is as it is what you learned while going through it. For example, perhaps you decided to take a paper route to earn extra money. Yes, you earned some money, but what did you learn? You learned to be on time and reliable in your delivery. You learned that what you did had value to others and how to collect for it. You probably gained in feelings of self-worth and contribution to your community.

Do not just consider the experience based on whether you were successful; instead, look to see what you learned from it. Whether you were successful in reaching your goal or not, you still learned. Even if you decide you never want to do it again, you will still have empathy for any paper deliverer who brings your paper for you. You will know to make different choices that are more suited to you.

Today I will look with new eyes on the experiences of my life. I will look to see what I learned from the process regardless of the outcome.

Dear God,

My life is so much more than I am able to understand. I know that you are in control and able to see the big picture. I trust that you want only good for me. Help me to learn from each experience in my life without judging the results.

Thank you, God!

What I learned from a recent experience:
_____
_____

July 29

A WINNING ATTITUDE

Attitude is extremely important in determining the direction of your life. If you have an attitude that says, "I can do it!" guess what—you will be able to do it. If you say, "I can't do that!" guess what—you will be defeated before you begin. Develop a positive attitude and it will serve you well.

There will be days when you do not perform as well as you could or perhaps your team did not play as well together as they sometimes do. Do not let this defeat you! Each day is a new beginning and a chance to play your best. Wake up with the idea, "Today is a good day to win!"

Today I will work on developing a positive winning attitude.

Dear God,

Give me a winning attitude even when things are not going well. My faith in myself will lead me on to success or to lessons that lead to greater successes.

Thank you, God!

What I say to myself to keep a good attitude is:

_____
_____
_____

July 30
SHAME

Shame is an emotion we feel when we do something that is not accepted in our society. We feel ashamed when we act in a way in which we show ourselves to be less than we really are. Shame is a cue that we need to change our behavior.

Shame is a negative emotion. It does not help you to rise up out of your situation. Acknowledge it and then ask God to help you let go of it and show you a better way.

Today if I find myself feeling ashamed about anything, I will release it to God's loving care. God will show me a better way.

Dear God,

There are times when I do something I regret. Show me a better way so that I can rise above this situation. I know you want only good for me.

Thank you, God!

I am sure God is pleased with these behaviors in my life:
_____
_____
_____
_____

July 31
SEEKING BALANCE

In all of life, there is a balance that must be achieved. For example, when it comes to feelings about yourself, on one end of the spectrum you may have total lack of self-esteem. On the other end, you might exhibit pride and arrogance. It is important to seek the balance between these continuums.

Another example is relationships. On one end, a person could be possessive, jealous, and controlling. On the other end, relationships might be free to grow to the point of being unguided or having too much freedom.

When the balance of male and female energies is examined, the balance is between the power and strength energies and the nurturing and loving energies...between logic and emotion.

Can you think of some other examples of the balance you must find?

_____
_____
_____
_____

Today I will seek a balance in everything I do. I will ask God's help.

Dear God,

Sometimes I do not realize when I am out of balance in some area of my life. When this happens, please call it to my attention and help me to correct the situation.

Thank you, God!

August 1
LEARNING FROM NATURE

When we observe nature, we are able to learn a lot about life. Notice that during winter there is an ebb. Everything is dormant. Many times in our life things seem the worst just before there is a breakthrough. We might even feel a sense of hopelessness. Then spring comes along and there is a flow. Everything begins to bloom and produce fruit. There is hope! It is beautiful again. In summer we often become complacent because everything is going so well. Everything is in full bloom. There is lots of activity. Then fall begins. Harvest is at its peak. Everything is most beautiful just before it goes dormant again. We gain our greatest wisdom just before we die. Watch the animals. How do they prepare for the ebb and flow in their life?

Today I will observe nature in all its forms. I will look for what it can teach me.

Dear God,

You are reflected in all forms of nature. You created everything. Help me to better understand how I fit into my world and what I can learn from nature.

Thank you, God!

When I observe nature, this is what I have noticed:
_____
_____
_____
_____
_____

August 2
GETTING SOMEONE ELSE IN TROUBLE

Sometimes in fights with siblings or friends, we are tempted to tell on them to get them in trouble. What would Jesus do? Perhaps if the friend or sibling was doing something life threatening, then it would be your obligation to tell on the person. However, if it's not, then you might want to ask yourself, "What part did I play in this? Was I treating everyone, including myself, with respect and truthfulness?"

Today I will be concerned only with my behavior. I am responsible for my own actions.

Dear God,

Help me to always be truthful in everything I do...to treat myself and others with respect. Help me to be there for others when they need me and to understand how I can change my behavior to avoid this situation in the future.

Thank you, God!

Situations in which to "tattle tale" is the right thing:
_____
_____
_____
_____

August 3
CIRCLE OF LIFE

> Everything the Power of the World does is done in a circle. The sky is round, and I have heard that the earth is round like a ball, and so are all the stars. The wind, in its greatest power, whirls. Birds make their nests in circles, for theirs is the same religion as ours. The sun comes forth and goes down again in a circle. The moon does the same, and both are round. Even the seasons form a great circle in their changing, and always come back again to where they were. The life of a man is a circle from childhood to childhood, and so it is in everything where power moves.
>
> <div align="right"><i>Black Elk
in Black Elk Speaks</i>[4]</div>

The circle in all cultures represents wholeness and unity. In the search for wholeness, we must achieve our own independence and find out who we really are. To do this we need the space to grow within the loving and supportive circle of our family and community.

Today I thank God for the circle of my family and friends. I ask God's guidance in becoming whole and realizing that I am a member of the large family of the earth.

Dear God,

Guide me to wholeness and unity. Help me to understand my place in the circle of life.

Thank you, God!

Action: Find out the sign language symbol for circle. Learn other words and concepts that use this same gesture.

August 4
CHOOSING FRIENDS

Friends are a wonderful gift from God. They help you through tears, fears, and joyful times. They have a listening ear. You share many of your experiences with them.

You will want to choose friends who will bring out your best qualities and will support you in your growth. Often you are called to be a role model for your friends and they to be a role model for you. This is good news if your friends have been raised by nurturing parents. It could also be bad news if your friends have low self-esteem and act out through their behavior.

Today I will choose to be around friends who are warm and friendly and allow me to be myself. I will choose friends who do not pressure me into doing things I do not feel comfortable doing. I will ask God for direction in choosing my friends.

Dear God,

I appreciate my friends. Please help me to choose good friends and to be a good friend to my friends as well. Help us to be good role models for each other.

Thank you, God!

The best things about my friends are:
_____
_____
_____
_____

August 5

*Today I give thanks to God
for increasing my awareness
of my inner world.
I can control my thoughts
and actions...*

*only I have
that
control.*

*Thank you,
God!*

August 6
WHO ARE YOUR TEACHERS?

You have teachers at school and you have teachers in daily life. It could be your brother or sister who teaches you about giving of yourself or the school bully who teaches you about unconditional love and forgiveness. Your friend may teach you to be a good listener. The store clerk may teach you about honesty. A stranger may help you out in a personal crisis and model helping others.

Today I give thanks to all of my teachers in school and in life.

Dear God,

Give me a new awareness of who my teachers are. Help me to learn my lessons quickly so they do not have to be repeated.

Thank you, God!

What I have learned from my teachers: _____

August 7
VIRTUAL REALITY

Sometimes it feels like we are living our lives with virtual reality glasses. The scenes, events, and situations keep changing, and God is nurturing our development by testing our thoughts, feelings, and actions until we mature into a spiritual being more like God. Life itself is the illusion, and we have more control than we think we do.

God is trying to train our thoughts, feelings, and actions until we come into our own power so that we will know how to handle it. God holds the knowledge of our true worth for us.

Today I will trust God's guidance in my growth.

Dear God,

The more I learn about you, the more awed I am that you love me so much. Thank you for your continued support and guidance.

Thank you, God!

I pray for guidance in these areas: _____
_____
_____
_____
_____

August 8
YOU ARE A TEACHER TO OTHERS

Who are you teaching lessons to in your life? What are you teaching your parents? What are you teaching your brothers and sisters...your friends, neighbors, anyone you meet?

You probably never thought of yourself as a teacher, but you are. You are probably teaching your parents unconditional love and forgiveness and helping them to be clearer in what they believe and stand for as they guide your growth. You are helping them to be teachers. You are probably teaching your brothers and sisters to communicate better, negotiate better, share, forgive others, and many other lessons such as these. Can you think of some other things you might be teaching others? List them here:

_____
_____
_____
_____

Today I will observe the lessons taking place between myself and others.

Dear God,

Help me to be a good teacher to others. Guide my actions. Help me to be clear on where I stand with my values.

Thank you, God!

August 9
WALKING INTO A BRICK WALL

Do you sometimes walk into a brick wall? Do you find yourself not learning the lessons you need to learn? For example, perhaps you cannot control your temper and get into fights at school so that you get into trouble with the principal? Or do you wait too long to begin studying for a test and then panic and cram. Perhaps you spread gossip and then wonder why you do not have many close friends.

Do you walk into brick walls or fall into a pit of your own making? What habits do you need to change in order to avoid the trap? List them here: _____
_____
_____
_____

Today I will examine my life to see where I may need to change my actions so I do not fall into a pit or walk into a wall of my own making.

Dear God,

You see all things. Guide me to see where I need to make changes in my actions so that I will have better results.

Thank you, God!

August 10
LACK OR PLENTY

How do you view your life? Is your cup half full or half empty? How you see yourself will make the difference. This reminds me of two sisters. The oldest sister always felt she could do anything, and she did. The next sister also was very talented, but she always compared herself to the oldest sister and came up short. Most of her life, she thought of herself as lacking. Guess what?! That is what her life reflected.

Do you see yourself as lacking in love from your parents? Then turn it around. Visualize yourself surrounded in their love. Do not waste time on being jealous of others. Instead see yourself surrounded in abundance and love. Appreciate what you have and it will only get better.

If you are feeling lack in any area, ask God to turn it around. Then let go—God can do all things. You can, too, through God.

Today I will examine my life for any place I may be feeling lack. I will team with God to turn it around.

Dear God,
I may not be able to control anyone else, but I can change how I look at something. Please help me to change this area in which I see lack: _____
_____
_____

Thank you, God!

August 11
THE POWER OF YOUR THOUGHTS

Many times what happens in your life is a reflection of your thoughts. An example of this is the hatred and violence carried over in generation after generation in Northern Ireland. Thoughts of revenge and hatred have permeated this area for a very long time.

Stand in front of a mirror. Make an angry face. Make a happy face...make a silly face. Remember that what you concentrate on will become more abundant in your life. If you frequently pout and think life is unfair, that is what will become more plentiful in your life.

What do you want to have more of in your life? _____
_____
_____
_____
_____

In front of that mirror, show what you want to see more of in your life. Now make it so.

Today I will remember the mirror. When I do, I will reflect what it is I want more of in my life.

Dear God,

Most times I am living my life unaware of what I am projecting. Please increase my awareness so that I will be more conscious of what I am bringing into my life with my thoughts and actions.

Thank you, God!

August 12
JUDGMENT

To make a judgment about someone means that we have preset notions as to how someone should act, behave, or look. It is important for us to be discriminating as to how we wish to interact with another based on our own beliefs. However, because others may not be raised with the same belief systems or standards, we should not judge.

By judging, we place a wall between ourselves and the other person. We determine that we are better than or less than the other person. This is wasted activity. It prevents us from trying to understand the other person. The other person may have something to offer us that we would pass by because we were not open to it. Get to know each person on his or her own merit. Try to see the flame of God within each person.

Today I will look deeper into each person I meet. I will not judge the other person and will stay open to what he or she has to offer to me.

Dear God,

You created each of us as unique individuals. Let me not forget that everyone contributes to our existence. Help me not to judge others before I have made an effort to really get to know them.

Thank you, God!

This is what I remember about a time someone unfairly judged me:
_____
_____
_____
_____

August 13
STRUGGLES

A struggle happens when we have to work through a situation in which we feel uncomfortable. We feel uncomfortable because the situation is new to us. We do not know how to respond. Perhaps our teacher assigns us work we do not understand or we are not sure what is expected of us. We might even fear that we won't be able to complete the task.

This is when we learn the most. We have to use our own creativity and brain to figure it out.

God will send us many struggles to help us learn our life lessons. We can try to solve a problem ourselves or we can ask for God's help. God loves to help. When we are most ready to give up and quit, we can choose to surrender to God's will. That is when a solution will come to our problem. With God as our partner, we will be able to handle any of life's struggles.

Today I will ask for God's help in solving my life's struggles.

Dear God,

When I am having a rough time at school or have had a bad fight with a friend, help me to find the answers to my problems. What do I need to do or learn? Help me to learn my lessons quickly.

Thank you, God!

Struggles I am facing for which I ask God's help:

_____
_____
_____

August 14
COMMITMENT

Commitment means you are willing to stay with a project or goal as long as it takes to reach completion. For example, perhaps you are taking piano lessons or playing soccer. Maybe you do not feel that you are very good at it. You want to quit.

You need to ask yourself what you might be learning from it besides just the skills needed for the activity. Teamwork? Coordination? In piano, you might be developing a musical background and appreciation that will help you with other instruments. It also teaches coordination and gives you time to be by yourself in quiet meditation.

Before you even begin any sport or lessons, you should set a length of time you are willing to commit to before you stop and reevaluate. If you stop too soon, you may have many lost opportunities. Everyone gets discouraged once in a while. It is important to learn how to work through those moments. That's how great musicians and athletes are formed.

Today I will commit to a length of time on any lessons or sports in which I participate.

Dear God,

Help me to stick to the commitment I am making on my sports or lessons. If I run into rough spots, help me to work through them.

Thank you, God!

The length of time for which I commit myself to (sport, lesson, or new activity) is: _____
_____
_____

August 15
DEVELOPING COMMON SENSE

Not everyone uses common sense. What is common sense? It results from applying what you have learned through school or other learning situations to your personal experiences. Using common sense allows us to get better results or to develop wisdom.

For example, Mark knows that when the temperature is below 32 degrees Fahrenheit it is cold and he may need protection. Common sense dictates that he take a warm jacket, gloves, and perhaps a hat, especially if he decides to go out later in the evening when the temperature drops even further. He may have learned that 32 degrees is cold, but it is experience that tells him how to dress appropriately.

Today I will look at the decisions I am making. Am I using common sense?

Dear God,

Guide me in making the best decisions I can make based on common sense and your wisdom.

Thank you, God!

Ask a parent or an adult you trust what common sense means to him or her. What is his or her answer? _____
_____
_____
_____

August 16
WHY DO I NEED TO GO TO SCHOOL?

There are several ways that people gain in wisdom as they journey through life. One way is through formal education. The other is through life experiences of relationships, situations, and events. As we learn, we gain in wisdom as Jesus did. We are able to better handle relationships, situations, and events with more positive outcomes. We keep ourselves out of trouble.

Today's world requires that people keep educating themselves in order to keep current and be able to earn a satisfactory living. The more educated you are, the more choice you will have and the more control you will feel over your life. Actually, after you leave school, you will find the real education begins on the job. Often you will even return to school to improve knowledge or skills in an area in which you are working.

Today I will acknowledge the good that education can bring to my life. I know that I will always continue to learn throughout my entire life.

Dear God,

Help me to appreciate the opportunities that you present for me to grow in knowledge and wisdom. Give me strength and perseverance to stay with it and do my personal best.

Thank you, God!

Today I am interested in learning about: _____
_____
_____
_____

August 17
NEED VERSUS WANT

Sometimes when we go to a store, we see many things we want. We are mesmerized by the displays of merchandise. It is easy to be convinced that we need to have things. Have you ever had the feeling that you just had to buy something and you did not care what it was? You browse until you find something you think you like. Later, you find it buried in your drawer almost unused.

There is a difference between need and want. When you need something, it means it is critical to your survival. When you want something, it means that you would just like to have it. Once you are clear on the difference between need and want, it is easier to make choices on how to spend your money.

When deciding whether to buy something, think about whether you have been saving for something special. Will buying the item be worth it if it takes that much longer to save for what you really want?

Today before I purchase anything, I will ask myself, "Do I need this or do I just want it?"

Dear God,

Help me to spend my money wisely. Give me an understanding of what my needs are and what I just want because I desire it.

Thank you, God!

What am I saving for? _____
_____
_____

August 18
BACK TO SCHOOL

Going back to school is usually an event that we anticipate, and it brings with it lots of questions. What teacher will I have? What subject will I be learning? What supplies do I need to get? What clothes will everyone be wearing?

In truth, we are always in school. Some training is just more formal than others. God is always directing our learning. We learn about getting along with other students and with our teachers. We learn self-discipline and study habits. We learn what rules work in the best interest of everyone.

Today I celebrate learning...all learning.

Dear God,

Thank you for all the opportunities and challenges you send my way. Thank you for all the teachers who guide and direct me. Help me to learn my lessons.

Thank you, God!

What I hope for at school this year: _____
_____
_____
_____

August 19
SERENITY PRAYER

Perhaps your mother is caught in traffic and unable to pick you up from practice on time, or two great opportunities are scheduled at the same time and you must choose between them. This is when the Serenity Prayer becomes helpful. It can be used every day of your life. It goes like this:

> God grant me the courage
>   to change the things I can,
> The serenity to accept those things
>   that cannot be changed,
> And give me the wisdom
>   to know the difference.

Many times when you run into a block in your life, you might ask yourself, "Can I change this? If not, please help me accept." You will notice your stress level go down immediately when you go through this questioning process. Try it.

Today I will ask myself to accept those things that cannot be changed.

Dear God,

Give me the wisdom to know when I can change something or when I must accept what is happening. Help me to trust that what is happening is what is supposed to be happening in my life right now and to look for the lesson.

Thank you, God!

Action: Memorize the Serenity Prayer. If this is difficult for you, write it several times or make a poster of it.

August 20

Today I give thanks for the wisdom, knowledge, and clarity of understanding that help me make good choices in my life.

Thank you, God!

August 21
STEALING

Have you ever gone on vacation and witnessed someone taking not only the complimentary items hotels provide but also the toilet paper and towels? That is stealing. Stealing means that you take something that is not yours.

Some gangs require new members to shoplift from stores as part of the ritual of joining the group. Shoplifting reduces profits from a store and causes all prices to rise to cover the cost of stolen items. Everyone pays. The same happens when people make false or inflated insurance claims. All the people then have to pay higher premiums in order to cover those who cheat the system. It is like stealing from your friends or brother. Jesus asks us to love our neighbor as ourselves. Could you steal from yourself?

Today I will show my respect for my fellow brothers and sisters by treating them as I would like to be treated. I will not steal or give acceptance to any discussion of taking something that does not belong to me. I will make restitution for anything I have taken and ask forgiveness.

Dear God,

Teach me true love and respect for my fellow brothers and sisters of God.

Thank you, God!

Ways I can contribute to my community:
_____
_____
_____
_____

August 22
LET GO OF THE OUTCOME

Many times when we pray to God, we tell God what we want to happen. We have an idea of how everything should happen even before it happens. By doing this, we limit God because to give us something else would interfere with our free will choice. Sometimes, we even try to bargain with God. God sees the big picture and knows what is best for us. Instead of telling God what we want, we should pray for what we want, or better, freeing God to give us something better. Then we will receive the very best God intended for us.

Another alternative is to pray to God for the best possible outcome for everyone involved. This gives God the opportunity to give good to everyone. It means that you need to "let go" of what you desire and trust that God will bring you what you wish or better.

There may be a time when you do not receive that for which you were asking. This means that it was not in your best interest. That is one of the reasons you need to allow God to determine your good. Then you will not be disappointed with what you receive.

Today I will trust in God's goodness and let go of any ideas that I have about what I want to happen.

Dear God,

You know what is best for me. You want to give me all manner of good things. Help me to trust you so deeply that I can just let go and know that I will receive what is best for me.

Thank you, God!

I'll let go and trust God to do what's best for all in this situation:
_____
_____

August 23
RELEASE OF FEAR

The opposite of love is fear. All manner of negative emotions (anger, stress, tension, jealousy, envy, rage, depression) are rooted in fear. Observe yourself. You will be able to identify fear-based emotions and feelings when they come up in you. You can release them through an exercise. Here is how you do it.

Ask God to be with you during this exercise. Feel where this fear is residing in your body. Is it in your stomach? Your intestines? Your head? Wherever it is, visualize bringing the fear up to your heart. See a little door open in your heart. Feel the energy leaving through that door. Do not judge whether it is good or bad, just feel it leave. Ask God to bring you into love again. See God's love pouring into the door in your heart. Give thanks. Your life will begin to change for the better. You will be clearing your body of fear. Soon you will experience better relationships, peace, hope, and joy on a regular basis.

Today when I get angry or feel slighted or experience any other negative feeling or emotion, I will release it through my heart.

Dear God,

I want to be in your love always. Help me to clear my body of all fear. Help me to recognize fear for what it is when it comes up in me.

Thank you, God!

August 24
LOOK FOR THE DEEPER LESSON

Everything you do is important. Therefore do your tasks consciously and with care, whether it is doing the dishes, taking out the garbage, or cleaning your room. Every act has a lesson. Remember in the movie "Karate Kid" when the master had the student repeat the same hand movement for long hours until he mastered it? You, too, learn from every movement. If the act were not important, you would not be doing it. Look for the deeper lesson.

Today I will do my chores and lessons with a conscious and caring attitude.

Dear God,

I do not always know why I am having to do some of the tasks and lessons I do. Help me to see what I am learning and to be a more conscious and caring student.

Thank you, God!

Deeper lessons I have learned:

_____
_____
_____
_____

August 25

*Today
God's direction
is guiding me.
I have nothing
to fear.*

Thank you, God!

August 26
GREED AND SELFISHNESS

Gift-giving times such as birthdays and Christmas really bring out our greedy side. We want more and more. When is it enough? Are we trying to find happiness in something outside ourselves? Truly, happiness can only come from inside. Sometimes it comes temporarily when we receive something we have wanted for a while. Most often it comes when we give ourselves to others.

Selfishness happens when we are overly concerned that we are not getting what should be coming to us. We try to take from others and are not willing to share. We are looking at the world through an attitude of lack. We think we are not worthy to receive our good.

God sees our true worth. God gives to all according to their need. Much of our good is waiting to be given to us. We need to trust that God will give it to us and convince ourselves that we are worthy. Once we see ourselves as worthy, we will begin to see others as worthy.

Today I will be mindful of all the good that God has waiting for me and remind myself that happiness comes from within.

Dear God,

When I am greedy, please remind me that you are always willing to give me my good. Help me to see my own self-worth and to realize my happiness within.

Thank you, God!

Give or share something of yours today. What will you offer to share or give? _____

_____

August 27
UNLIMITED POSSIBILITIES

God has given us a world with unlimited possibilities. This means that our current situation can change in the future. We can do or be anything we want to do or be if we just set a goal and work toward it. The more we focus on our goal, the more it becomes real for us.

Ask for God's guidance in achieving your goals. When you do, teachers and helpers will appear in your path. The right opportunities will come to you.

If an obstacle comes in your path, do not just throw up your hands and give up. Instead, pray to see a way around or through it.

Today I will adopt as my motto: "Where there's a will, there's a way." I will look at the unlimited possibilities in my life.

Dear God,

Thank you for the unlimited possibilities in my life. Do not let me get discouraged by small problems and obstacles in my life. Instead help me to see the unlimited possibilities for solving them.

Thank you, God!

Action: Read about Jesse Owens growing up. Think about how he opened his mind, heart, and spirit to unlimited possibilities:

_____
_____
_____

August 28
LISTEN TO YOUR INNER GUIDE

All of us have an inner guide that tries to keep us walking in truth. Some people think of it as the angel and the devil. We want to impulsively do something that is not in our best interest, and the inner voice says, "If you do that, _____ will happen." Our ego is the little devil trying to tempt us to do something about which we feel uncomfortable. It tries to convince us that we are more powerful than God. When we listen to our ego, we end up disillusioned and blaming God because the situation did not go our way. In reality we were responsible.

When we listen to our inner voice (the quiet voice of God), we choose our best course of action. When we listen to our ego, we often get in trouble. For example, John wants to go to the movies with friends. He cannot reach his mother to let her know where he is going. The ego says "Go ahead. She will understand." The inner voice says, "Maybe you should wait until you get permission. You know your parents will worry if they do not know where you are or who is with you." What will you do?

Today when I have to make choices, I will listen to my inner guide.

Dear God,

Sometimes I get carried away with the moment and make poor choices. Help me to remember to listen to my inner guide before making any decisions.

Thank you, God!

I am listening to the quiet, small voice of God in me. Here's what it says: _____

August 29
ARROGANCE

Arrogance is displayed when people act as if they are better than others or they are the only one who can provide a better solution or decision. They think their voice counts more than the voice of others. An arrogant person is usually not open to others' ideas or opinions.

People who are arrogant are usually insecure. They are not open to the love or support offered by others and try to stand alone. This hurts these people the most. They do not realize that we are all one in God. They often do not see God in themselves or others. They do not feel God's love. They have a hard time connecting to others.

When you run into an arrogant person, instead of feeling put down by the person, visualize him or her surrounded in God's love and light. Treat the person with kindness and love. See God working through him or her. Step back and watch miracles happen.

Today I surround with love anyone who is arrogant or difficult.

Dear God,

When I run into arrogant or difficult people, help me to see you in them. Help me to stay centered in you and treat them with kindness.

Thank you, God!

How did you feel when you visualized others surrounded in love?

_____
_____
_____
_____

August 30
UNCONDITIONAL LOVE

Unconditional love means that regardless of what you do or say, you are loved anyway. This is the way God loves us. God allows us freedom of choice. Sometimes our choices are bad, but God is always willing to forgive us. When we love unconditionally, it means that we do not give judgment on what we or others do or say; we love each other as children of God. This does not mean we have to agree with what others do or say, it only means that we see God in them and love them as one of God's children.

Jesus said, "Let he who is without sin cast the first stone." We all make bad choices at times. God wants us to learn from it and move on. If we hold on to our past and refuse to forgive ourselves and let go, then we stop our own growth. We are called to support each other in our growth and realize that we are all one in God. We are loved and forgiven unconditionally.

Today I will not judge myself or others. I am loved unconditionally by God, so I will love myself and others unconditionally.

Dear God,

Thank you for loving me so much. Help me to learn about unconditional love and to use it with myself and others.

Thank you, God!

I let go of these mistakes and trust God to help me grow from them:
_____
_____
_____

August 31
LOVE RELATIONSHIPS

During adolescence, crushes often are referred to as "puppy love." Mature love cannot be experienced until a person has discovered who he or she really is. This does not really begin until after you are out on your own and free from parental supervision.

Many people think they can complete themselves through another person. This simply is not true. Witness all of the failed marriages and relationships. Another misconception is that you can change another person. You cannot change anyone unless that person is willing. Accept the person as he or she is.

You must find completeness or wholeness in yourself first. As long as you feel things can only be better if you have a love mate, you will not find a right match. Once you have determined you can be complete in yourself, then a relationship will be more successful. Relationships take work—caring for another and supporting the person in his or her growth. It also means developing good communication skills. Do not be in a rush to get married. Give yourself time to decide if it will work for you.

Today I will nurture any relationships I have, keeping in mind that I am still getting to know myself. Until I know who I am, I cannot know someone else.

Dear God,

Teach and guide me in my relationship choices. Help me to learn from each one. Help me to know when I am ready for a true commitment.

Thank you, God!

These are traits I hope my mate will have, so I will begin developing them in myself: _____
_____

September 1
YOU ARE BEING GUIDED

Your life is not one accident or coincidence after another. Everything happens for a purpose. God is directing your life. God has guides and angels watching over you.

When you have a question or something you wish to change about yourself, ask your angels to help you and meditate. Ask them to bring you solutions to problems or to increase your creativity and understanding. You have many resources at your disposal if you will only use them.

Do not look to another person to provide the answers for your life. Look inside yourself. What does your inner voice say? God dwells within you. God's guiding emotion is peace. What choices make you feel peaceful?

Today I will look inside myself for answers to life's questions and dilemmas.

Dear God,

Sometimes I get confused by all the messages I receive from TV, teachers, parents, and friends. Help me to be clear in what I believe and what my truth is. Help me to take responsibility for my own answers.

Thank you, God!

What choices make you feel peaceful?
_____
_____
_____
_____

September 2

HONORING PEOPLE OF ALL OCCUPATIONS

Labor Day is a day celebrating all people who work. This includes people of all different occupations. Each person performs a service that contributes to the overall good of us all. If your car does not work, a good mechanic is invaluable. If you are ill, a doctor is important to you.

When workers takes pride and joy in doing their job, it shows. The quality of their work is excellent. They love what they do. When people do not like what they are doing, they are likely to provide shoddy quality or service.

As you look at what you might like to do with your life, choose something not because it brings greater money or prestige but because you can give it from the heart. Work is an expression of your giving of yourself.

Today I will look at what I enjoy doing for others and ask God's guidance in choosing a career.

Dear God,

Guide me in choosing work or a career that is guided from the heart. Let my work be the best expression of myself.

Thank you, God!

I give thanks for people in these occupations:
_____
_____
_____
_____

September 3

I am loved by a love so great. There is nothing I can do that will separate me from the love of God.

Thank you, God!

September 4
OPEN YOURSELF TO OTHERS

Many people find it difficult to open up to others with their problems. When you are in touch with your Creator, you become aware that you are like everyone else. Everyone has similar problems and bad days. Ask God to help you see yourself as you truly are. Surrender yourself to God's help and the best outcome will occur. God sees the truth of who you really are. God helps you to see solutions to problems when you ask for help.

God often reaches you through others. Do not be afraid or embarrassed to share your difficulties. You will find that others have suffered the same situations too. Sharing helps to lessen the pain and comforts those involved. It often puts your concerns in perspective. By sharing your problem with others, you can get insights into how to handle your situation. You are ultimately responsible for the outcome of your situation.

Today I will share my problems with someone I trust. I will surrender to God's intervention.

Dear God,

I know you love me unconditionally. You see the bigger picture. I surrender my problem (_____) to you. Guide me in the best solution or help me to accept where I am right now.

Thank you, God!

September 5
PRIDE

Pride is a quality that can encourage your best efforts. It can also be a quality that creates a barrier between you and receiving the good you have coming to you. For example, pride may prevent you from forgiving another, resulting in a loss of friendship, peace, and goodwill. Pride can prevent you from learning something when it stops you from asking questions you need to ask because you are afraid to admit you do not understand. Pride may keep you from asking for help when you need it. Consequently, you might feel alone and isolated instead of loved and supported.

There is a delicate balance between taking pride in something you are doing or creating and having pride become a destructive quality. Can you think of a time when your pride was constructive for you?

_____
_____
_____
_____

How about when it was destructive for you? _____
_____
_____
_____

Today I will be mindful of using my pride in a constructive way.

Dear God,

I wish to be aware of pridefulness. Help me to use it in a constructive way. Make me aware when I am being destructive with it so that I can make changes.

Thank you, God!

September 6
PRAYING WITH YOUR FAMILY

When you pray together as one voice, you have much power. Pray with your family, who knows and loves you. You can support each other by praying for each other. Establish a prayer basket. Place your desires and wishes in the prayer basket and then give them up to God.

Another idea is to ask each member to contribute to a group prayer. Imagine a gold thread connecting all of you to each other. Send your love to each person. Say one thing you appreciate about each family member. Have each family member continue in turn. This will strengthen the family bond.

Plan a family prayer service and invite all family members. Ask God to be present with you as you plan and carry out the service. Use candles and music to set a tone of sacredness. Have all family members contribute something they wish to share...a favorite prayer or poem, story or song. Then end with a group prayer of gratitude to God for all your blessings. Have all family members share a blessing for which they are particularly grateful.

Today I will pray with my family.

Dear God,

Help me to support my family and myself through group prayer, appreciation, and gratitude. Let me see our prayer at work through you.

Thank you, God!

September 7

Today I choose to listen to others with compassion and empathy. Their problems remain theirs to solve, but I can comfort them with my love and attention.

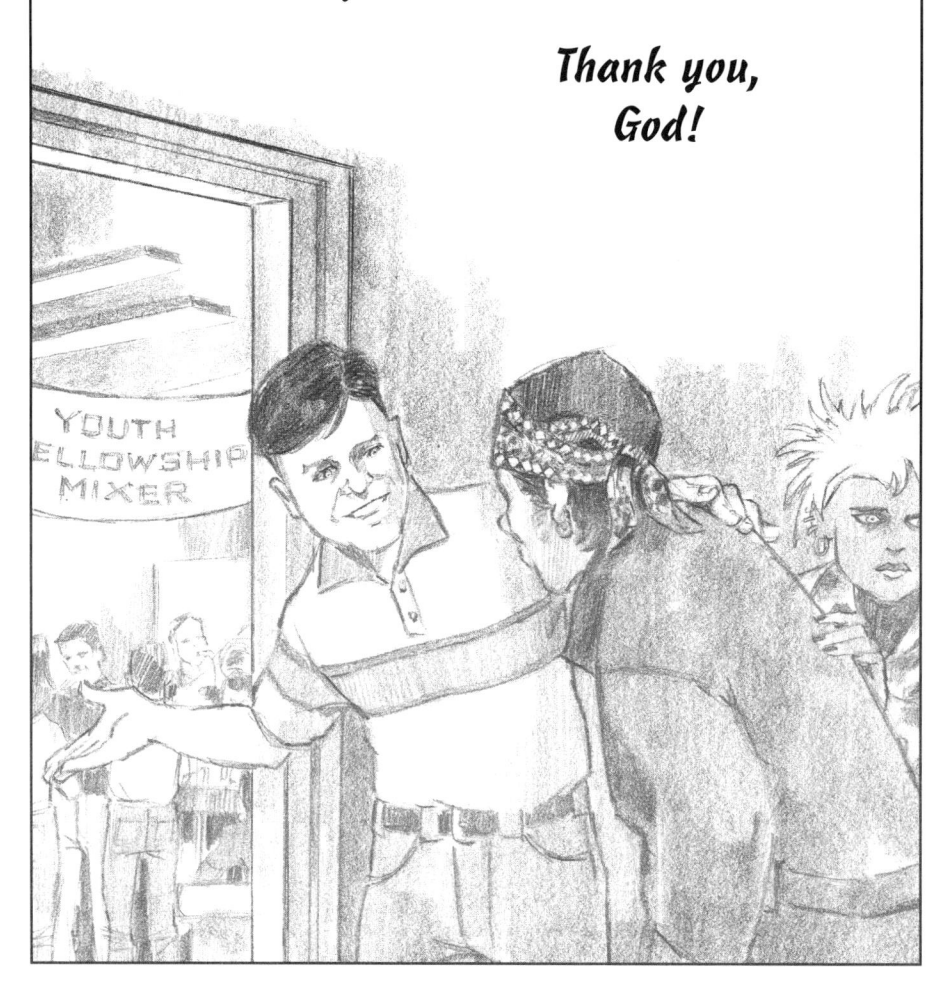

Thank you, God!

September 8
GRANDPARENTS

Grandparents hold the wisdom for us. They have already been through many of the same struggles we have and probably some different ones.

Ask your grandparents to tell you about how life was for them when they were growing up. What were their struggles? What were their failures? What would they do different if they could?

Honor your grandparents for all the experiences and wisdom they have gained.

Today I will search out the wisdom my grandparents hold for me. I will honor them for all that they have experienced in life.

Dear God,

Thank you for the courage of my grandparents. Help me to listen carefully to what I can learn from them.

Thank you, God!

If your grandparents are not available, ask another older adult the questions above. What did they say? _____
_____
_____
_____

September 9
TRYING TO MOVE TOO QUICKLY

There are times when I try to move too fast. Perhaps someone is putting pressure on me to take care of something I should have taken care of a while ago. So I rush. In the process, tension and crisis usually result. Something gets dropped, broken, or left behind by accident.

Other times I may have a craft kit or project. If I get in too big of a hurry and do not read directions, something goes wrong on the project or it does not turn out as beautiful as it could have been. This is true of life in general. When we try too hard to hurry the timetable, it may backfire on us. Everything requires thought and some pre-planning. Then we have to go through the steps to completion. We have to give each step our full attention. Only then will the final result be the best that it can be.

Often the best way to plan is to note when a project needs to be started, not just when it is due.

Today I will take the time and do the steps needed to complete any task or project. I will give it my full attention, effort, and patience.

Dear God,

I know I cannot be older by wishing it; I have to live each day to get there. This happens with any projects or efforts I make on a daily basis, too. Develop in me the patience and determination to take each step to completion.

Thank you, God!

_____ (date) is when I need to start on: _____
_____

It is due: _____

September 10
TIMING

Timing will be an issue all of your life. You have probably experienced timing considerations already. For example, you tried to ask for something from your mother while she was talking on the phone to your teacher. She probably asked you to wait or come back later. Maybe you have already figured out that it is not a good idea to ask for a favor or privilege right after disobeying a house rule.

God also has timing considerations. There may be times that you want something, but God knows you are not ready for it. You may even feel frustrated and anxious. Accept God's will for you. Know that God wants only good for you. Timing means that you have to practice patience and self-restraint. Trust in God.

Many times our rainbows come after a dark, stormy period. Know that when you are experiencing a time of darkness, the light is right around the corner. The key word is patience!

Today I will use my inner guidance on issues of timing. I will practice patience and self-restraint.

Dear God,

I have had a difficult time with timing. Guide me and develop in me patience and self-restraint. Most of all, give me hope and trust in you.

Thank you, God!

Ways I can use timing to help others today: _____
_____
_____
_____

September 11
BEING CYNICAL OR CRITICAL

Have you ever run across someone who can only see the dark side of life? If you say "It's a beautiful day!" they say, "It's going to rain!" Cynical people are distrusting of other's motives and are pessimistic about life and their future in general. Cynical people are not aware of the good God wants to bring into their life. Because they can only see the dark side of life, they are not open to the lessons they are receiving.

Pray for cynical people to be able to see themselves as God sees them. Pray that they might be opened to their good. Form a picture in your mind of them surrounded in God's light and love. Ask God to protect you from their dark view of life. It is easy to be dragged into their pessimistic outlook. Pessimistic people limit themselves the most. By calling attention to the dark side of life, they bring more of it into their life. Do not make this mistake! Keep a positive, God-filled outlook.

Today I will keep a positive outlook on life. If I run into any pessimism, I will ask God to turn it around through Divine Love.

Dear God,

Help me to clear myself of being pessimistic or cynical. Let me be a model to others of how to live a positive and whole life.

Thank you, God!

The glass is half full, not half empty! Here is a situation I am going to view optimistically: _____
_____
_____

September 12

SETTING BOUNDARIES

Being able to set boundaries around us is important to our continued growth. Boundaries protect us from being run over by others. Boundaries keep us from going in the wrong direction and help us to achieve our inner balance. Most of our boundaries are mental and emotional. Of course, physically we do not want anyone touching us in a place or way that we cannot accept. The emotional and mental boundaries are more difficult to establish.

Have you ever noticed that a person who makes more of a fuss always seems to be served better and faster than others? That person voiced boundaries. When you can state what you will do or not do, you are setting boundaries for yourself. When you find yourself in a difficulty in which your time is being abused by someone else, ask yourself, "What boundaries do I need to set for myself to regain my balance?"

Today I will meditate on boundaries. I will ask God where I need to establish my boundaries.

Dear God,

This idea of boundaries feels new to me. It means that I have to see my own self-worth. It means that I have rights over my time and myself. Guide me in setting loving boundaries.

Thank you, God!

Boundaries I need to establish: _____
_____
_____
_____

September 13
TRUE MEASURE OF A PERSON

When you are young, it is possible to look up to someone you admire and be in awe. This means you put the person on a pedestal and think he or she can do no wrong. No matter the age, whether they are rich or poor; black, white, yellow, or red; male or female...no matter how famous, other people function exactly like you. They have emotions, get lonely, get sick, have family; learn life lessons, and make mistakes. They feel guilt, elation, shame, joy, and sadness, and they put their pants on one leg at a time just like you.

Never think of anyone as better than or less than you. Everyone is at a different place of development. Everyone is unique. Everyone is your equal. Know yourself and your own value. Appreciate others for what they offer and how they treat people. We are all children of God.

Today I will treat everyone as my equal. I will treat them as I want to be treated. As my equal, no one can put me down, nor can they place me on a pedestal.

Dear God,

Help me to see my own worth. I will not put anyone above or below me. We were all created in your image.

Thank you, God!

Imagine your favorite actor or actress brushing his or her teeth. How does that make you feel? _____
_____
_____

September 14
CONVERSING WITH OTHERS

When you wish to make conversation with someone, focus your attention on that person and not on yourself. Ask questions about the person's favorite music, books, movies, or activities. When you think of the other person instead of yourself, you will not need to work at conversation. It will flow easily.

At the table be sure to choose conversation that is not controversial or offensive or that will not cause an argument. Stay away from politics or religion as a topic because people are usually quite passionate about their beliefs and someone may not agree with you. Polite etiquette suggests no arguing while you are eating.

You may wish to connect with a person or group of peers who like to discuss different topics freely without judgment. Sometimes by doing this it helps to clarify your own beliefs and feelings.

Today I will choose someone I do not know well and strike up a conversation with that person.

Dear God,

Sometimes when I talk to someone I do not know well, I feel shy and unsure. I do not always know what to say. Help me to focus on others and get to know them better. Help me to forget about myself and my shyness.

Thank you, God!

Today I will start a conversation with: _____
Some topics I might discuss are: _____
_____
_____
_____

September 15
COMPARISONS

When we compare, something has to be better and something has to be less. This is true whether we compare people, situations, or something we own. It is better not to compare.

Have you ever been in a situation in which you were perfectly happy with something you owned until someone came along and criticized it? Then you no longer liked it. Or have you ever had a friend come to visit, and although you knock yourself out to show him or her a good time, all your friend can do is compare what you have with what he or she has back home? Somehow it makes your efforts feel diminished.

Accept whatever comes your way. It is neither more nor less—it just is. Accept.

Today I will be on my guard against comparing.
I will accept everything that comes into my life as it is.

Dear God,

Help me to accept and learn from every experience. Thank you for all the good that comes to me. Let me be aware if I start to compare or in any way diminish others.

Thank you, God!

I accept these situations in my life:
_____
_____
_____
_____

September 16
IMPULSIVENESS

Are you impulsive? People who are impulsive can be swayed by emotion. They act as if they are driven. They might get an idea in their mind and feel drawn to carry it out immediately regardless of what might have been going on before.

Impulsive people might think they just have to have that beautiful pair of shoes in the store window even though they have plenty at home…or they just have to finish reading a book even though it will be 4 a.m. before they finish and there is school the next day. An impulsive person might forget all about the test the next day that he or she should study for and instead join friends on the spur of the moment for a movie. We all make choices. Some choices are made more consciously than others. Think through to all of the consequences of your decisions. "Yes, maybe I can go to the movies if I use study hall to study for the test." Meet your obligations and then plan to have fun.

Today I will "be conscious" when I need to make choices. I choose to meet my obligations and also have fun.

Dear God,

Help me to be fully there when I make choices. Help me to clearly see all alternatives and consequences.

Thank you, God!

Consequences of a decision I am making: _____
_____
_____
_____

September 17
DISABILITIES

Have you ever broken an arm or leg? Have you watched someone on crutches try to get around carrying a book bag and opening doors? It throws the person off-balance, yet he or she is determined to do it.

When a person is disabled, it means a body part might not be working as it was meant to, but the person's spirit is in fine order. People with disabilities are not separate from us but have learned to make adjustments and accept that it might take them longer to do a task that others take for granted. People with disabilities learn special lessons on acceptance, patience, compassion, persistence, and determination. Disabled teens have the same wants, needs, and fears as other teenagers.

Today I will get to know the spirit of a disabled person. If I have any prior beliefs or myths about disability, I will seek to find the truth.

Dear God,

I take many things for granted. Help me to treat all people equally and be a true friend. Help me to be compassionate with others and myself.

Thank you, God!

Often, blind people have exceptional hearing. What adjustments have you had to make with an injury?

___
___
___
___

September 18
TRADITIONS AND RITUALS

Traditions and rituals teach us about the past so we can learn from it. They also tell us about important milestones we have reached in our development. The Jewish faith has a ritual called Bar Mitzvah to celebrate a young man reaching young adulthood. Some cultures celebrate when young women menstruate for the first time, indicating that the girl has become a woman. Being able to get a driver's license, turning 21, graduation, and wedding ceremonies are all traditions and rituals that mark milestones in a young person's life. Each milestone achieved required some preparation and is noted by your support group (family, friends, and community) through ceremony and celebration.

In modern times, because of busy lifestyles, many traditions have fallen by the wayside. They are needed, however, to let young people know the seriousness of each step in their development. What are the traditions and rituals in your family? Discuss them with your parents. What skills or preparation is necessary? List them below.

Tradition: Preparation:
_____   _____
_____   _____
_____   _____

Today I will become more mindful of the importance of traditions and rituals.

Dear God,

What can I learn from rituals and traditions? I have taken them for granted and sometimes feel they are silly. Help me to see their importance in my life.

Thank you, God!

September 19
BEING SHY

Shy people do not believe in themselves. They are not sure what they have to offer and feel separated and fearful of others' thoughts and reactions to their input. They imagine others as being better or greater than they are. People are shy because they are fearful. They view themselves as coming up short of others' expectations.

Being shy is a choice. Pray for help in seeing your true worth as God sees you. Choose to participate in activities that will build your confidence and self-esteem. You will find that when you open up and share your fears, others will relate to you better. You will be able to see the similarities between you and others rather than the differences. Smile frequently—smiles open doors.

Today I will work to overcome my shyness by reaching out to others. If I see someone who is shy, I will smile and encourage the person. We are all here to help each other in our growth.

Dear God,

I make my life more difficult than it really needs to be. Open me up to experiences that will build my self-confidence and self-esteem. I choose to let go of my fears.

Thank you, God!

What was the shy person's reaction to your smile?
_____
_____
_____
_____
_____

September 20

ALL SAINTS' DAY

All Saints' Day is a day to remember all souls who have lived before us. It is a time to reflect on what we learned from them. What courage did they demonstrate? What qualities did they best project? What would you not like to have repeated?

Think of relatives or friends who have passed over to the spirit side. What did they teach you? You might wish to discuss this with your parents. _____
_____
_____
_____

Choose an autobiography of a famous person. What did that person teach you? We can learn much from our ancestors and those who lived before us.

Today I will take time to appreciate and learn from the struggles of those who lived before me.

Dear God,

Thank you for all I can learn from those saints who went before me.

Thank you, God!

September 21

TREASURES OF HEART AND MIND

Only you can control what is in your heart and mind. If you live with fear, what you will experience in your life will be a reflection of that fear. If you live a life of love and belief in God, your life will reflect love and all the good God has to offer. Trust that God will care for you just as Jesus was cared for. Listen for God's inner guidance. Then your life will be full. You will not fall victim to the hopelessness and futility others experience. You will look for the lessons you are to learn and grow in appreciation for all the good God brings into your life.

Today I will appreciate God and all the good God brings to my life.

Dear God,

When images of fear control me, help me to turn them around to loving images. Grow my awareness so that I will always turn to my Source of Love.

Thank you, God!

Treasures God sees in my heart and mind:

_____
_____
_____
_____

September 22

HARVEST TIME

After the seeds have been sown and the plants mature, it is time for harvest. It is a time of celebration when the harvest is good. God has been working with all souls over the millennia of time. He has been maturing everyone and plans a good harvest.

We were born in this world as lights in the darkness. The darkness cannot overcome the light. When we allow our light to shine, we are allowing God's light to shine through us. God's light transforms the darkness. Even now it is possible to see the fruit of God's light shining through each of us in our world. You can see God's good happening now.

Today I will look for evidence of God's good happening in my world.

Dear God,

You are the light of my being. You offer me hope eternal. Help me see your good happening in my life. I wish to be part of your harvest.

Thank you, God!

Good things happening in my life: _____
_____
_____
_____
_____

September 23

*Today when the problems
of the world seem
overwhelming,
I will remember
that God is in charge.
I do not have to solve
all of the world's problems.
Instead I will place
them in God's
loving Care.*

*Thank you,
God!*

September 24

TREATMENT OF FAMILY MEMBERS

Your family is where you receive the most teaching regarding building relationships. Often we treat our family members worse than others because we feel more free to let our guard down around them. Take a close look at your family relationships now.

Who is teaching you your greatest lesson now?
_____

Who do you treat poorly?
_____

How do you plan to change that?
_____

When did you last tell your family how much you appreciated them?
_____

How will you tell them now?
_____

Is there any bad feeling between you and anyone in your family?
Circle: Yes   No

Ask God to help you let go of this feeling now. Release it to God's care. Give thanks. Be grateful for your family and all of the opportunities you receive to learn love and forgiveness.

Today I thank God for my family. I will treat them as I would treat a best friend. As I change how I look at my family, our relationships will improve.

Dear God,

Thank you for my family. If there is a way I can change myself to improve the relationship I have with my family, please help me to do so. I know I am only responsible for myself and my own thoughts, feelings, and actions.

Thank you, God!

September 25
YOUR MOOD AFFECTS OTHERS

Once in a while people wake up in a foul mood. They may snap at anyone who comes close to them. As their day progresses, they will complain loudly because nothing seems to go their way. In the process, everyone is affected. Others will try to stay as far away as possible. Because these people are not at peace in their heart and mind, they project this lack of peace to others. Think about how this feels.

Whether you are the one with the bad start or are on the receiving end, it helps to ease the situation if you just acknowledge that you had a bad start. "I feel like I got a bad start." "Please give me some space until I can regain my good humor." Or offer empathy: "Are you having a tough day?" "I hope you feel better soon." Often, once the bad mood is acknowledged, the person can choose to improve and most likely will. Sharing empathy helps to take the edge off the bad start.

Today I choose to be at peace. I do not have to continue a bad day if I choose otherwise.

Dear God,

Today I got a bad start. I choose to be at peace. Please help me to turn this around and reflect your peace to others.

Thank you, God!

How my mood affected others today: _____
_____
_____
_____

September 26
GROWING IN RESPONSIBILITY

When you were 5 or 6 years old, your parents probably asked you to clean your room and to clear the table after meals. Sometimes they even helped you. Then as you got older, you were given other responsibilities such as feeding pets, washing dishes, and so on. You are growing in responsibility when you are able to plan the time when you will do a task and then follow through without being told or supervised. When this time comes, you will be more confident in yourself and your abilities. You will be afforded more privileges.

Your parents will not need to guide you as much once you are capable of acting and thinking on your own initiative. That means you do not have to be told. When you can think and act on your own, your parents will have more confidence to let you go farther on your own. You will have more freedoms. This happens with God also. When you lay a good, strong foundation of values in your life, you will find more freedom and more inner joy, peace, and love. Fewer restrictions are needed.

Today I will work on growing in responsibility...trusting in the good things to come.

Dear God,

Help me to grow in responsibility and to learn my lessons quickly. I want to experience your inner peace, joy, love, and freedom.

Thank you, God!

Here are some freedoms I have earned since 2 years ago:
_____
_____
_____

September 27
LABELS

We often give ourselves labels. "I'm stupid." "I'm fat or skinny." "I'm slow, clumsy." "I'm a clown" ...popular or unpopular, and so on. Once we label ourselves or another, we often work to make it true. Because we are always changing, a label may be true one day but be inappropriate a week later. It is best not to give ourselves or others labels. Do not participate when others give labels. Accept everyone as he or she is today. Do not judge unless you wish to be judged. Forgive others if you are labeled.

Today I will refuse to participate in labeling myself or others.

Dear God,

If I begin to participate in any labeling, help me to see it. Do not allow me to label myself or anyone else.

Thank you, God!

Try to visualize yourself as God sees you. What are you like?

_____
_____
_____
_____

September 28

*Today I feel
the Joy
of the
Universe
shining forth
through me.*

*Thank you,
God!*

September 29

DEALING WITH CHANGE

We are always in a state of change, but we just do not recognize it. Often, when something changes drastically in our lives, we are fearful. We do not know what the future will bring. This is when having faith that God always does things for our good will help us through difficult times. God wants only good for us. Once we have asked God to have our needs met, we need to trust that God will provide that or something better.

If we have to move, for instance, we are probably afraid we will lose our friends. We might be unsure where we will be living and where things are. Later, we will discover that not only do we have a better home with a bigger bedroom for us but that we like our new friends and school even better.

Today I will learn to trust in God's desire to have only good for me. When change occurs, I will have faith in God's plan even though I do not know the exact outcome.

Dear God,

Even though my life is in change, I know that what you have in mind will be even better for me. I will trust in the Lord's mercy. Help me to grow into the person you want me to be.

Thank you, God!

Changes I am facing:
_____
_____
_____
_____

September 30
CHEATING

Cheating happens when you use someone else's answers for a test. It's possible to study with someone and do homework cooperatively. If you are doing so only to get answers from someone, then it is cheating. Cheating is when you don't do your own work. The only loser will be you because you will have never learned the material.

Cheating is like telling a lie...it can get you in big trouble with others. When the time comes that you need that information, you will not know it.

Today I will do all my own work. I will do my best and face the consequences if I do not do well. I will see what I can do better next time in order to improve.

Dear God,

Please help me to do my best work. Teach me the best study habits so I will do well. If I don't do well, Lord, show me what I can do next time to do better.

Thank you, God!

My good study habits are/will be:

_____
_____
_____
_____

October 1
BEING OPEN TO NEW PEOPLE

Today there was a new person in my class. I did not know what to say to the person. Being the new person in a group can be difficult. When someone decides to befriend a new person, it gives the person confidence and makes him or her feel welcome. Smiles are one way of opening doors. Another is asking questions of the other person, such as "What do you like to do in your free time?" or "What are your favorite subjects (books, music)?"

Be open to new people in your world. Your world will be constantly changing as you continue to grow. Sometimes you may find yourself being the new person on the block. You may want a new friend, too,

Today I will be open to being a friend to someone new. I will be warm and welcoming.

Dear God,

Help me to be friendly and open to new people, ideas, and experiences so that I can grow.

Thank you, God!

Share something with someone new today. Take a meal to a neighbor, send a note of welcome or thanks to someone at your church, or offer to study with a new student. What are other ways to reach out to "new" people? _____
_____
_____
_____

OCTOBER 2
GUILT

Guilt is a feeling that makes you feel bad about yourself...usually because of something you did not do, something you wish you had done better, or something you wish you had not done at all. For example, maybe you forgot to get a card for your mother's birthday or you did not take care of someone's game that you borrowed and lost. Now you feel guilty about it. Guilt is wasted emotion. It is a clue that you need to change your actions next time.

By forgiving ourselves and others and walking the path of truth, we can make guilt go away. Walking the path of truth means being honest with ourselves and others at all times.

Today my actions will reflect only truth and what is right and just.

Dear God,

I need not have guilt as my partner if I am true in my thoughts, words, and actions. Help me to walk the path of truth, fairness, and justice.

Thank you, God!

I forgive myself for whatever I did that made me feel guilty. Here's how I will change: _____
_____
_____
_____
_____

October 3
SINGLING OUT SOMEONE

When there is a group of young people, frequently one person will be singled out to be the butt of jokes and ridicule. Often the person is picked on for things that everyone in the group has done, but they cannot face it and so they assign it to "the scapegoat." That person may be the last student to enter the class after school has started, or maybe the person is someone who does not fit in well. In either case the person feels like an outcast and feels no one likes him or her.

You can help alleviate this situation by getting to know the person better. Do not participate in cruel jokes or remarks at someone else's expense. Is that how you would want to be treated? Stand up for the person and point out his or her contributions or good points to the others. Be the person's ally!

Today I will be a friend to anyone I find being ridiculed or picked on.

Dear God,

Help me to see clearly when I am participating in any behavior that singles out someone for ridicule. I ask your forgiveness. Give me courage to be a true friend to everyone.

Thank you, God!

What would you like to be forgiven for? _____
_____
_____
_____

October 4
FOLLOWING THROUGH

Today you told your mom you would take out the trash, but you never got around to it. That is called not following through. Following through means that after you have said that you would do something, you do it.

Following through is required throughout your life. A person who does what he or she says is often referred to as being "as good as his or her word." You will know you are growing up when you are able to follow through on a regular basis. Then you will begin to gain the respect of adults and your peers. It also will help you to get the jobs you want.

Today I will concentrate on following through on anything I say I will do.

Dear God,

It's difficult to follow through. I would rather visit with friends or play a game. Help me to learn this important quality so that others will be able to count on me.

Thank you, God!

Today I followed through on:

_____
_____
_____
_____

October 5
CREATE YOUR OWN DESTINY

You do create your own destiny. God has granted us "co-creator" status. When you focus your attention long enough on something you want to do, everything starts to change to make it happen. Teachers come, finances are planned, studying begins, and soon you are doing what you wanted to do.

What if you change your mind? That's OK! Nothing you ever do will be a waste. The experience will contribute to something you are doing later. Be clear in your goals and team up with God.

Today I will ask God's help in making me clear about my future goals. I will trust that nothing will be a waste. I'm right where I belong now.

Dear God,

Help me to be clear about what I want to do. Be my partner and guide me on my path.

Thank you, God!

Here's the vision I have for my life: _____
_____
_____
_____
_____
_____

October 6

MONEY DOES NOT BUY FRIENDS

It is fun to treat friends now and then when we have some extra money in our pocket. When we try to throw our money around too often, we will soon find that money does not buy true friends. Some friends only follow the money trail. When it dries up, they disappear.

True friends will be with you through good times and bad. They will stay with you during times when you are not popular. True friends like you for being you. They will spend money on you, too, when they have it.

Today I will look at my friends. Are they the kind who will stay with me through good times and bad? Will they bring out my best qualities or my worst?

Dear God,

I want to be discriminating about my friends. Help me to choose friends who like me for being me and who will bring out my best. Help me to bring out their best, too.

Thank you, God!

Two things I can do today to bring out the best in my friends:

1. _____
   _____

2. _____
   _____

October 7

HAVING VISION

> Vision without action is merely a dream.
> Action without vision just passes the time.
> Vision with action can change the world.
> *Joel Arthur Barker*[5]

Having vision means being able to picture where you want to be and under what conditions. When you are young, it is difficult to have vision. There are many choices available to you, and you need time to explore them.

Vision is necessary in picturing how you want your life and world to be. Various cultures have spent much time trying to obtain a vision of life purpose. It requires quiet contemplation. You can obtain your vision also through meditation or giving yourself time to be alone. Ask God to help you with your vision. No one can give you a vision. It must come from inside you.

Today I will set aside time to be alone in the quiet. I will ask God for my vision.

Dear God,

Show me how I can make this world a better place. What is my life's purpose? I will wait for the signs you give me.

Thank you, God!

When I get quiet, close my eyes, and look inside, this is what I see:
_____
_____
_____

October 8
OUR EFFORTS MAKE A DIFFERENCE

Sometimes when we have concerns about something (for example, pollution), we do not know where to start to do something about the problem and feel like our efforts cannot make a difference.

Think about what happens to a glass of water when a drop of dye is placed in it. At first there is no change. But as each new drop is added, the color spreads more and more through the water until all of the water is the color of the dye. This is what happens with our efforts. First one person takes the first step and plants the thought that change is possible, then others join that person, and suddenly a powerful energy is produced. Then change actually begins to take place.

Today I will ask God to develop in me the faith to take the first step. I will have faith that things will happen for the good of all, even if I cannot see it right this moment.

Dear God,

Develop in me faith and courage of conviction. Help me take a stand for the things I feel strongly about, even if I do not see immediate results. Help me to believe in the power of myself working with you as my partner.

Thank you, God!

The first step I take today is: _____
_____
_____
_____

October 9

BUILDING VERSUS BURNING BRIDGES

Throughout your life there will be situations that do not work out. For example, perhaps you have a paper route. One day you decide you do not feel like getting up early. You sleep in without calling your route manager. The customers begin angrily calling, wondering what happened to their paper.

By not accepting responsibility and by not communicating, you have just burned a bridge. You may never be able to work for this company again, and they will not give you a good reference for any other job. If you had taken care of your responsibilities, you would still have a job and a good reference for future jobs.

If you choose not to continue with this line of work, the responsible way to maintain good relations is to call your route manager. Explain that this is not something you wish to do any longer. Give two weeks' notice and ask for a reference for the work you have done. This type of communication maintains goodwill. At a future time, if you decide you want a paper route again, your manager would probably hire you again.

Today I will be careful to build bridges of good relationships, whether in sports, school, clubs, activities, work, or at home.

Dear God,

Help me to see when I am in danger of burning bridges. Help me learn the skills of responsibility and communication to maintain good relationships with others.

Thank you, God!

Other ways I can build bridges: _____
_____

October 10

*Today I give thanks
for the power of choice.
I can choose my own outcome.
Even that can be changed
if I so choose.*

Thank you, God!

October 11
NEEDING CREATIVE INSPIRATION

When I need creative inspiration, I can ask God for help. All ideas originate from God, so by asking God for inspiration, we are tapping into Divine Intelligence, which is God. You first define the situation and then be still and wait for the ideas to flow. Have a paper and pencil ready or be at your computer to write them down.

Today, when I need ideas on how to handle a problem or on creative ideas for making something, I will ask God for inspiration.

Dear God,
You are the source of everything. I wish to ask for inspiration on

_____
_____

Inspire me with ideas.

Thank you, God!

October 12
ACCEPTANCE

Many times when things happen, we deny it instead of accepting it. Until we find acceptance of the truth, we cannot change. For example, you might say, "I'm only a little late with my homework" or "I'm just a little out of shape." When someone says they are "a little of ____," do you think they have the motivation to change? No. Can you be "just a little dishonest?" No!

Ask God for the strength to accept what is going on and the clarity to see what must be changed.

Today I will accept whatever is going on in my life. I will ask God to help me see my part in it and to make the changes I need to make.

Dear God,

You see everything in truth. Help me to accept those things I cannot change and give me strength to change the things I can change.

Thank you, God!

Today I am asking God to help me accept:
_____
_____
_____

October 13

GOD LOVES CHILDREN

"Truly, I say to you, whoever does not receive the kingdom of God like a child shall not enter it." Mark 10:15

The disciple Mark was quoting Jesus. Jesus was telling the people that they have to be like a child to enter the kingdom of heaven. Why? Children are accepting. They love everyone. Children are curious and want to learn more about why things are as they are. They ask questions. Children forgive easily. Life is simple to a child. Children find pleasure in the smallest things. Children live in the present moment. Jesus also said, "Let the children come to me; do not hinder them; for to such belongs the kingdom of God." Mark 10:14

God loves all Creation. God wants us to love and forgive easily and to find joy in the small things. God wants us to be accepting of ourselves and others. We should be curious about God and about how the laws of the universe work. We should turn to God with our troubles and worries.

Today I will continue to hold on to those childlike qualities that God treasures—love, acceptance, trust, forgiveness, and an inquisitive nature.

Dear God,

Help me to always be childlike in my love for you. Help me to keep those qualities you treasure.

Thank you, God!

Childlike qualities in me that God treasures:
_____
_____
_____

October 14
WHOSE PROBLEM IS IT?

In our effort to help others, we often confuse their problems for ours. Suddenly we can be overwhelmed with problems that are not even ours. When this happens, ask yourself, "Whose problem is this?" You can help others to see their alternatives but allow them to make the choices and own the problem.

You cannot fix everything for others, and they cannot fix things for you. You can be supportive of the decisions they make. If you cannot be supportive and think they may hurt themselves (as is the case when a friend chooses to use drugs), then you can tell them that you do not agree with their choice, and because you care about them, you must tell them that you do not agree. Then pray to God that they will be able to see themselves and their actions in truth. Do not judge your friend or the situation, because it may be just the lesson God provided for your friend to turn his or her life around.

Today I will ask myself, "Whose problem is it?" when I am discussing anyone's challenges. I will not judge what is going on.

Dear God,

Help me to be clear who owns the problem. I wish to be a supportive friend. Help me to be clear about when I am offering choices or trying to take over and fix the problem.

Thank you, God!

I will give this problem to God today: _____
_____
_____
_____

October 15
BURNING THE CANDLE AT BOTH ENDS

Picture a candle burning at both ends. What happens? It burns down quickly, doesn't it? This is what happens to our energy when our activity level gets to the point where we are not getting enough rest and downtime. We burn out. When we are overtired, we are not able to think clearly and we consistently make poor judgments. We may become more accident-prone. Our emotions will not be under the normal control, so we may get angry easier or be irritable. Is this how we wish to be? If not, it may be time to seek balance.

It is often the practice of young people to party until late and then get up early for an athletic event...watch a TV movie until late and then get up early for school...or procrastinate in studying for an exam and then study all night the night before the exam. Research has proven that the mind becomes confused and does not function well without adequate rest. You might wish to examine your habits. Are you burning the candle at both ends?

Today I will seek balance in the amount of activity, recreation, and downtime I need.

Dear God,

Give me the wisdom to know when I am overdoing it. Please protect me from hurting myself or others through lack of judgment or balance.

Thank you, God!

How much rest I will get today: _____
_____
_____

October 16
LIMITING YOURSELF

You limit yourself when you tell yourself "I'm not good enough to do ____". You limit yourself when you operate from fear. You are a child of God. God does not make junk.

One way you can discern whether you are operating from fear or not is to ask yourself, "Does this come from love? Is it delivered in love? Does this make me doubt myself or my abilities? Am I stopping my opportunities to grow because of fear?"

Make the decision now to remove fear from your life. Every time a thought comes up that is not from love, acknowledge it and ask God to change it to love. Then restate the way you think.

Today I am ridding myself of fear. God wants me to be all I can be. I will release all limiting thoughts, feelings, and actions.

Dear God,

I limit myself when I think negatively or from fear. I want to be all you created me to be. Help me to let go of all limiting thoughts, feelings, and actions.

Thank you, God!

Let your imagination soar. What are some of the amazing possibilities God is preparing me for? _____
_____
_____
_____

October 17
DEAD RIGHT

Being right seems to be a goal for many young people. You can be "right" in your assumptions or theory and still not win. If you damage a friendship, being "right" will not help. In traffic a driver may be "right," but if he is killed proving it, he still did not win. There are many times in life when you will have to decide whether being "right" is important or not. Everyone has a different view of truth. Decide what your truth is but honor others' truth also. Agree to disagree if that is the best thing to do in a situation.

Today I will observe whether I need to be "right" in my interactions with others. What will it cost me?

Dear God,

Sometimes I do not realize when I am forcing my beliefs on others or when "being right" is more important than the damage that could happen to relationships I have with others. Awaken me to those moments so that I can make the changes I need to make.

Thank you, God!

Whose job is it to judge right and wrong? _____
_____
_____
_____
_____

October 18
DIFFICULT RELATIONSHIPS

Every now and then we run into people who are very difficult to deal with, and they cause us no end of anguish. Maybe it is a bully or someone who finds joy in putting you down or ridiculing others. Often, when we encounter someone like that, the inclination is to stay as far away as possible or to attack. Do not dwell on the person's behavior. Instead, pray that God will help you see that person as he or she really is. Think about whether God has sent that person to teach you something. What is the lesson? If this is the case, once you have learned the lesson, the situation may disappear or you may have made a new friend. Remember, we were made from love and God wants us to show love to others.

Today I will look for what I am to learn when I encounter a difficult person. I will ask God to bless the person and help me see the person's true self.

Dear God,

When I am having difficulty appreciating another person, help me to see the person as his or her true self. Help me to look for the good in others. Teach me to love unconditionally.

Thank you, God!

What have you learned from dealing with a difficult person?
_____
_____
_____
_____

October 19

GOD LOVES YOU AS YOU ARE RIGHT NOW

You are perfect just as God created you. Believe it! You are learning and growing. God's love is unconditional. Nothing will make God stop loving you. God created you.

Today I love myself and honor myself as a creation of God. I will treat myself in a loving manner.

Dear God,

Help me to know the magnitude of your love for me and for all your Creation. Fill my heart with love, joy, and peace.

Thank you, God!

Look in the mirror. Repeat today's affirmation and prayer as you look at yourself. Smile! You are wonderful right now!

October 20

Today I will take a walk in Nature and learn from the plants and animals.

Thank you, God!

October 21

GIVER OR TAKER?

Are you a giver or a taker? Do you give of yourself to those around you or do you take from them? The question is not about money; it is about your time, attention, and caring. Take stock of yourself.

• In what ways do you give of yourself? _____
_____
_____

• In what ways do you take from others? _____
_____
_____

• How can you do better? _____
_____
_____

Today I will take a good long look at myself. I will work to make sure I am a giver as well as a taker.

Dear God,

I need nurturing from parents and teachers. There are lots of ways I need help right now, but as I get older, help me to see the many ways I can give back to others. Help me to be there for others now.

Thank you, God!

October 22

COMMUNICATING FEELINGS

You have a fight with your sister. She took something of yours without asking. When do you speak?

1. FIRST, OBSERVE WITHOUT EVALUATING: **"When I see you wearing my sweater,"**
2. HOW YOU ARE FEELING ABOUT WHAT HAPPENED?: **"I feel frustrated"**
3. WHAT NEEDS, DESIRES, WISHES, AND VALUES ARE CREATING YOUR FEELINGS?: **"Because I value respect and trust."**
4. REQUEST THAT WHICH WOULD IMPROVE THE SITUATION WITHOUT DEMANDING[6]: **"Are you willing to agree that in the future you will ask me before you borrow my clothes?"**

There is no blaming or accusation with this method. Everyone feels better about themselves.

Today I will reflect on my own needs and feelings. Then I will make my request for what would make me feel better in the future and ask for agreement. Next I will respectfully listen to whatever response I hear, and tune into the feelings and needs of the other person, so that out of that connection, we can find a way for everyone's needs to be met.

Dear God,

When I am unhappy, help me to figure out what I am feeling. What need do I have that has not been met? I do not wish to judge, criticize, or blame anyone. Help me to use this method in resolving conflicts with others. Help me to learn to communicate my feelings and needs more effectively.

Thank you, God!

Action: Think of a recent argument. Write down how you might have responded using the technique mentioned above.

October 23
RETICENCE OR SPEAKING DIRECTLY

There are many different methods of speaking. Some people are reticent. This means that they keep all their thoughts and feelings to themselves and rarely speak of them. This makes it difficult for others to get to know them or communicate with them because they always have to guess what the reticent person is thinking.

Another style is speaking directly. This type of person says just what he or she is thinking. Sometimes in the process, others' feelings get hurt because the truth can be hurtful. However, everyone always knows how they stand with this person.

The opposite of the direct speaker is a person who speaks in a circular motion. Circular speakers are afraid to tell a person what they want the person to know, so they tell everyone else instead, knowing it will get back to the person they really wanted to tell in the first place. The problem with this method is that it involves everyone else in the situation.

What other methods have you observed? The best approach is to be honest yet tactful, meaning you try not to hurt others' feelings if you can help it. Try to envision how the other person will react. Is it really necessary to tell the person what you think, or would it be better left unsaid?

Today I will be conscious of my communication method and that of those around me.

Dear God,

Teach me to communicate in a way that is honest, loving, and kind.

Thank you, God!

Practice saying something difficult in each of the four styles.

October 24

HONORING PEOPLE OF ALL RELIGIONS AND CULTURES

God created us all. God is so huge a concept that we are unable to define all that God is. We could all agree, however, that God is bigger than all of us, because the concept of each of us is held by God. There could be as many ways to worship God as there are people. There could also be as many ways to live and interpret life as there are the number of people God created. This means then that we need to honor all ways of living and worshipping God.

We are called to honor all cultures and all religions as ways of God's expression through us or our expression through God. In the act of honoring, seek to understand others and not just to be understood. We are all one family in God. We must seek to get along as one big family. You can do this by first seeking to know and understand your own family. Then seek to know and understand your community, nation, and world.

Today I will honor all religions and cultures by seeking to know and understand my family, community, nation, and world.

Dear God,

Help me to be open to all ways of worshipping you and all ways of expressing life. I wish to have a greater understanding of other cultures and religions. Please provide the teachers and experiences to make it so.

Thank you, God!

Another culture or religion about which I will learn something today is: _____

What I learned: _____
_____

October 25

HANDLING DISAPPOINTMENT

There are times when something you really wanted did not happen. Perhaps you auditioned for a part in a play and did not get what you wanted, or maybe you tried out for basketball and did not make the team. We all experience disappointment.

Instead of berating yourself and saying to yourself, "You are not good enough," think about what you are good at doing. Acknowledge that this time you did not make it. Will you try again? Think about your successes and try to stay with that thought and feeling of success. Handling disappointment is critical to future successes.

Today I will reflect on how I have handled past disappointments and think of how I will react in the future.

Dear God,

I feel bad when something I have anticipated does not come through. Teach me to handle disappointment so that I do not defeat myself from having future successes.

Thank you, God!

I am good at these things: _____
_____
_____
_____
_____

October 26

*Today
I give thanks
for the bounty
given to us through
Harvest time.*

*Thank you,
God!*

October 27

PROCRASTINATING

To procrastinate is to put off doing a task until the last minute. Have you procrastinated in cleaning your room or doing your homework? Procrastination is knowing you have something to do but instead thinking of other things you would rather do.

In order to overcome procrastinating, you must prioritize. This means that you make a list of those items you need to do. Then you mark the most important tasks. You proceed in doing the tasks by their priority, or how important they are. This requires self-discipline.

Where do you often procrastinate? _____
_____
_____

Make a list of your tasks and prioritize them by their importance. How did you feel when they were done? As you grow up, you will be required to prioritize your responsibilities. You will find that you have more free time once you quit wasting time by procrastinating.

Today I will prioritize my responsibilities and take charge of my life.

Dear God,

Sometimes I just cannot seem to get my tasks done. Develop in me the ability to prioritize and complete my tasks.

Thank you, God!

October 28
OWNERSHIP

Who is the real owner of your things? Your home? The land you occupy? In human terms, your parents may be owners or perhaps there is a landlord involved. In reality we are not owners...we are only caretakers. God is the creator and owner of all. Humans have come and gone over eons of time, but the land has continued to be and thrive despite human intervention. In the Bible, Genesis 1:28 says that God made all creatures and gave man dominion over them. This means God gave man power to rule over them. Do we actually own earth, our animals, and so on? No! We have the responsibility to be guardians of them and make them prosper as God did at Creation.

How good of caretakers have we been? How good of a caretaker are you over the things for which you have been given responsibility?

_____
_____
_____

Today I will take measure of how good a caretaker I am over the land, animals, and things for which I have responsibility.

Dear God,

We as the human race have forgotten our responsibilities as you laid them out for us as caretakers of the earth. Awaken me to my responsibility. Awaken us all.

Thank you, God!

October 29
BEAUTY IS SKIN DEEP

From where does beauty come? What is beautiful to some is not to others. People who are handsome or beautiful radiate a certain spiritual essence. They have confidence in themselves. They seem to have an abundance of energy. Good grooming helps to make the person more appealing, and a smile is most important. Clothing only helps. It does not make the person but is a form of self-expression. True beauty comes from within.

Some people will go to great lengths with surgery, cosmetics, and fitness training to improve the outside. But no matter how many changes people make on the outside, if they do not like themselves on the inside, they never reflect their true beauty.

Today I will look at myself in the mirror. What is it that brings out my essence? I will ask my friends or parents what about me appeals most to them. Their answers will likely reflect my inner qualities.

Dear God,

This is the time when outer beauty is often stressed. Do not let me lose sight of the fact that my inner spirit is where real beauty originates.

Thank you, God!

Record your answers here:
_____
_____
_____
_____
_____

October 30
LISTENING TO OTHERS

Listening to another is very difficult at times. We get so involved thinking of what we wish to say that we miss what the other person is saying. To truly listen to another means that we must give the person our undivided attention and let go of our brain chatter.

When there is a break in the conversation, nod or say, "umm hmm" or "Oh, then what happened?" to give the person an opportunity to continue. Do not say anything else at the same time. Keep eye contact with the person. This is one way of showing your love and caring for that person. The person will walk away feeling very good because you have just given him or her your whole focus.

Today I will "listen" to my friends and give them my undivided attention.

Dear God,

I learn the most when I am open and receptive to what is being said. Oftentimes I am too busy trying to talk and am not receptive. Help me to be more open and receptive to my friends, others, and you.

Thank you, God!

Action: Select the person for whom you will practice your listening skills. Ask about his or her day, then remember to maintain eye contact. Give the person your full attention and encourage further talk if he or she pauses.

October 31
HALLOWEEN

Historically, Halloween was the celebration of the eve of All Saints Day, a day to remember those who have lived before us. Today Halloween is a day to dress up and pretend to be someone other than who you normally are. It is a day for creativity, frivolity, and "trick or treating" for sweets.

While you are "trick or treating," be sure to do it with a group of friends you can trust to respect others. Any "tricks" that result in property damage or taking something that belongs to others are not acceptable.

Read an autobiography of someone of the past to get an idea of their struggles and triumphs. You can learn from the lives of others. What did you learn? _____
_____
_____
_____

Today I will enjoy the creativity, frivolity, and companionship of Halloween. I will be sure to show gratitude and respect for others while I am "trick or treating."

Dear God,

This is sure to be a fun day. I look forward to the school parties and "trick or treating" with friends. Help me to take the time to reflect on those who have lived before us and see what I can learn from their lives.

Thank you, God!

November 1
THE END MAY NOT JUSTIFY THE MEANS

You may have a task to do. You have to rake the yard. You would like to get your brother to help you. The goal is a raked yard. The "means" is the method you choose to get the job done. In this case you want your brother to help you. Some people might try to physically force their brother to help. How do you think he would feel? Others might try to blackmail their brother into helping. How well do you think that would work? How would he feel toward you? Some people would bribe or manipulate him into doing the work. How do you think he would feel? A loving sibling might use this method: "Adam, I have to rake the yard. It is a very boring job for me and lonely, too. Would you come and keep me company while I work? Maybe you could tell me jokes, too." How do you think Adam will feel? Do you think he might even pitch in and help?

When you have a goal, there are many ways to get there. A spiritual person will choose a method that honors and respects all those involved. Can you recall a recent experience in which you had something you had to accomplish? What means did you use to accomplish your goal? What other means could you have used?

Record your answers here: _____
_____
_____
_____

Today I will reflect on the means I use to accomplish my goals. Is my method loving, respectful, and honest?

Dear God,

Give me the insight to realize when the means I am using to accomplish my goal is not the best it could be.

Thank you, God!

November 2
SPREAD THE JOY!

Collect 10 jokes and share with friends.

Do something unexpected for someone you love today.

Smile frequently.

Sing a happy song.

November 3
DREAMS

During dreams we are often working out situations that we act out later in our daily lives. If you go to bed with a problem on your mind, you may find that a solution comes to you upon waking. Though your body is asleep, your mind continues to work throughout the night.

In the Bible, Joseph, the son of Jacob, is able to interpret the meaning of dreams for the King of Egypt. Also, Joseph, the father of Jesus, receives a message from God in his dreams telling him that he should flee with Mary and Jesus to Egypt for safekeeping.

Dreams are one of the ways God speaks to us. You can become more aware of your dreams by telling yourself you want to remember your dreams. Keep a paper and pen handy by your bedside so that when you awaken you can record anything you remember about your dream. What did you learn? The more you write down your dreams, the more you will get from them. Ask God to help you understand them.

Today I will pay closer attention to my dreams.

Dear God,

Help me to understand my dreams. I wish to let go of any anxiety I have about _____
_____

I give it into your care.

Thank you, God!

November 4
BRAGGING OR BOASTING

People brag about something they think is better than someone else's. "I have the best pitch in the league." People who boast or brag speak with an excessive pride. "My school is better than yours." Though they do not realize they are doing so, they often put down someone or something else in the process. Bragging and boasting is not appreciated by others. It can be irritating and make others feel bad about themselves. No one wants to be around someone who brags frequently.

It is nice to feel good about something you do well or be associated with others who do well. When you are good at what you do, others will notice. You do not have to boast or brag. If you wish to comment on others' achievements, you might say, "I am proud of my school. They are particularly good at _____." This tells others of your school's specific achievements without you taking credit for something you had no part in.

Today I will be mindful of those times I start to boast. Is there another way I can rephrase what I want to say that will not be offensive?

Dear God,

I do not wish to offend others through boasting. Help me to see clearly when I am beginning to boast.

Thank you, God!

What can you say about others' achievements? _____
_____
_____
_____
_____

November 5
ABUSE

No one has the right to hit or verbally abuse another human being. We are all children of God. People who physically or verbally abuse others usually feel very bad about themselves.

Keeping a secret about the abuse does not help and often perpetuates it. Only by bringing it out in the open can everyone receive help.

Today I will tell myself I am loved by God and do not have to accept abuse nor will I give it. If I witness abuse, I will report it to someone who can help. If I am being abused, I will tell an adult I trust.

Dear God,

Thank you for loving me. Guide me to the right people who will help stop abuse.

Thank you, God!

This is how I pray for victims of abuse: _____
_____
_____
_____

November 6

KEEPING UP APPEARANCES

When a person tries to keep up appearances, it means that he or she is making something appear different than it really is. For example, Billy brags about his father and how great he is. In truth, Billy's father left the family and ignores him. Billy keeps up the appearance that his father cares for him. Another example: Jennifer wears beautiful clothes to school and makes a big deal out of how she looks. No one has ever been to her house because Jennifer does not own anything but the clothes she wears and barely has enough food to eat. Jennifer keeps up the appearance that everything is great instead of reaching out to others for help.

People try to keep up appearances when circumstances are different than they wish they could be. Perhaps pride, envy, or some other emotion gets in the way of them facing the truth. Do you have an area in your life that appears different than it really is? _____
_____
_____
_____

Ask God to help you face it.

Today I choose to live my life in truth. There will be no more false appearances.

Dear God,

I wish to live my life in truth. Help me to bring my life in line with how I wish to live it. If I cannot control the circumstances, then help me to accept them and make the best of the situation.

Thank you, God!

November 7
PUTTING YOURSELF IN A BOX

You put yourself in a box when the rules and regulations by which you live become so restrictive that they limit your growth. For example, Josh refuses to play with other people who are not of his nationality. He limits his opportunity to learn of other cultures and make new friends.

Alana is afraid to take part in sports because she thinks she will get injured. She misses out on good exercise, interaction with friends, and the joy of being part of a team. Nathanial comes from a wealthy family. He refuses to associate with anyone who is not of his stature. Nathanial misses out on experiencing the breadth of life. His fear keeps him from developing close relationships with others. The only thing he sees is how much wealth a person has.

Look at your life. Do you have rules that you impose on yourself that keep you from experiencing all of life? _____
_____
_____
_____

Today I will examine my life for rules I impose upon myself that limit my growth and experience.

Dear God,

Help me to set boundaries for myself that protect but do not limit my growth and experience of life.

Thank you, God!

November 8

KEEPING A JOURNAL

Keeping a journal is a form of communicating with God and learning more about yourself. Perhaps something has been bothering you. Your journal is a place in which you write down what is bothering you. In the process of writing out your feelings and talking to God, you are able to come to a solution or to work out your feelings.

Our feelings are the hardest part to understand. They may feel like a tightness in our stomach or a feeling of confusion. Because feelings are not really visible, it helps to write in a journal about them.

The more you write in your journal, the more in touch with your feelings and thoughts you will be. Some people like to write in their journal after meditating. Then they can catch thoughts from meditation. Others like to write when something is confusing or bothering them. Another opportunity to write might be when you wonder how you are feeling about a topic or an issue. By putting all your thoughts and ideas on paper, you get a feeling of how thoroughly you have thought a matter out and where you stand on it.

Today I will write in my journal about _____
_____
_____
at (time) _____

Dear God,

I want to know myself better. Help me to learn the art of keeping a journal so that I may get in better touch with my thoughts and feelings.

Thank you, God!

November 9

BLACK AND WHITE VERSUS GRAY THINKING

When people use black and white thinking, it means they draw a line on a certain issue and no matter what the circumstance, they make no exceptions. They will not bend on their thinking or cross the line.

People who are gray thinkers also will draw the line on an issue, but certain circumstances might permit them to change the line. For example, if a poor child was starving and stole food, how would these types of thinkers respond? Black and white thinkers would throw the young person in juvenile detention regardless of the circumstance because they do not believe in stealing. If you steal, there are consequences.

Gray thinkers do not believe in stealing either, but in this instance they might choose compassion and try to help the young person before a career in stealing becomes the result. Gray thinkers look beyond the act to the circumstance that caused it.

Today I will examine my thinking. Am I a black and white thinker or a gray thinker?

Dear God,

Help me to model Jesus and have compassion for others. I may not condone their behavior or believe as they do but I still love them as a child of the Creator.

Thank you, God!

A situation in which I was a black and white thinker:
_____
_____

A situation in which I was a gray thinker:
_____
_____

November 10
SEEING THE BIGGER PICTURE

Perhaps you want a special dress for a school dance, but your parents tell you they do not have the money. What they did not tell you is that your dad might soon be laid off his job. Or maybe you want a new playground at the school. It will involve raising lots of money. However, the school is also trying to raise money for a new gymnasium and feels it cannot focus on two projects at once. Your project is deferred.

Many times when we want to act on something, we do not see the whole story. Not until we ask lots of questions do we finally begin to see all that is involved. When you want something you are not getting, remember that God sees the bigger picture. Ask God to help you see the bigger picture too. Ask for the best possible result to happen.

Today I will try to see the bigger picture. I realize that I am not the nucleus of the world. There is a bigger picture waiting for me to see it.

Dear God,

So that I don't fuss because I am not getting my way, help me to see the bigger picture and to realize that I am part of a much bigger whole.

Thank you, God!

In what situations are you not getting your way? What are some possible "big pictures" to explain why this is so?

_____
_____
_____
_____

November 11

THINK HEALTHY

Winter is a tough time for good health. What can you do to bring the odds in your favor?

- Think healthy
- Get enough rest
- Get consistent exercise
- Eat good foods, especially fruits and vegetables. Remember that too much sugar lowers your immune system.

Doctors say that germs are spread most often by hands and in the air. If this is so, washing your hands before putting them in your mouth is important. Also, wash them after going to the rest room. When you wash your hands, be sure to wash under fingernails and between fingers up to the knuckles. Always cover your sneezes and turn your head away from others. Use a tissue or handkerchief if possible to cover coughs and sneezes.

Today I will practice good health habits and think healthy.

Dear God,

Many times I take my body for granted. I know that my actions can influence the overall health of my body, as well as the bodies of others. Give me the will and discipline to ensure good health and well-being for myself.

Thank you, God!

These are other things I can do to stay healthy:
_____
_____
_____

November 12
INTEGRITY OF ACTIONS

Integrity is a word that describes a person who always acts with the highest level of behavior even if no one is watching. A person who acts with integrity is a person who will try to find the owner when he or she finds a lost wallet on the sidewalk. A person with integrity will not tell lies or spread gossip. When he or she agrees to do something, it is as good as done. A person with integrity is true to himself or herself.

Integrity comes from the word *integrate*—all parts working together in harmony. A person with integrity cannot say he or she believes in something and then act in a way that is inconsistent with that belief.

Today I will act with integrity.

Dear God,

Help me to understand the word "integrity" and to be an example of it to myself and others. I may have to grow into it, Lord. Be patient with me.

Thank you, God!

I will be true to myself today when I _____
_____
_____
_____
_____

November 13
LIVE LIFE IN MODERATION

You have probably heard parents, friends, or relatives discuss living life in moderation. What does this mean? There is a balance to be achieved in everything we do. If you eat too much food over time, you will be faced with weight problems and resulting poor health. If you eat too little food, you will be shorting yourself of nutrients that ensure proper operation of the body.

When you listen to music too loudly, you risk damaging your ear drums and losing your ability to hear. Too much reading all at once may fatigue your eyes. Too little will make you uninformed. Too much exercise can cause fatigue and injuries. Too little means you will not have proper body tone; you may gain weight and be subject to depression. Exercise raises the amount of oxygen and endorphins in your body. Endorphins make you feel happy. The lesson to be learned here is to live your life in moderation.

Today I will look at areas in which I may need to bring my habits into balance.

Dear God,

Clarify for me those areas in which I need to live life more moderately. Develop in me the discipline to do so.

Thank you, God!

To live in moderation today, I will _____
_____
_____
_____

November 14

MOUNTAINS VERSUS MOLE HILLS

Once in a while our problems will seem overwhelming. We make them seem even bigger in our minds by dwelling on how bad they are. Nothing can help us put things in perspective faster than visiting a homeless shelter or some other place where people truly have overwhelming problems. Talk to a friend or a group of friends about your problems. Soon you will see that they have the same kind of problems as you.

Ask God to help you see the truth of your situation. Ask God's help on a creative solution. Better yet...let go of the problem. Put it in God's hands and allow God to work things out. God will do this through you. Allow enough quiet time for the solution to come.

Today when a situation or event comes up that seems overwhelming, I will ask God's help in putting it back in perspective.

Dear God,

You see all things as good. Help me to see them as you do. Help me to see the gift you are bringing me today in this situation. Help me to keep it in perspective.

Thank you, God!

A mole hill I once thought was a mountain is: _____
_____
_____
_____
_____

November 15

USING COLOR IN YOUR LIFE

Colors have a great impact on our world. Some colors elicit an emotional response from us. Green and blue have a relaxing effect. Yellow and red bring us to full alert and may even help sharpen our minds. Black is the color that reflects the least amount of light. It feels heavy and depressing. It is also bold when used in small amounts. Subdued colors say, "I do not want to be noticed." Bright colors say, "Look at me. Here I am."

In the spiritual world, blue and violet are healing and transforming colors. If you are feeling ill, envision blue light surrounding your body. This envisioning is the same as prayer. See yourself getting well. Ask God for healing energy.

If you are experiencing a difficult situation, envision a violet transforming flame surrounding the situation and all people involved. As you are doing this, ask God to transform the situation to its highest good through Divine Love.

Today I will look at how I am using color in my life. What am I saying about myself? I will use the spiritual colors blue and violet in times when healing and complete change are needed.

Dear God,

Thank you for the gifts of sight and color. Help me to see all the ways colors can be used to enhance my life. Help me in learning to use the healing and transforming colors.

Thank you, God!

My favorite color is _____
because _____

November 16

*Today I give thanks
for all the challenges and
opportunities in my life....
They are there
for my growth.*

*Thank you,
God!*

November 17

STUDY THE PAST TO ENSURE A BRIGHTER FUTURE

If you only study or memorize facts and figures, you will not learn anything from history. Instead, try to learn from mistakes that were made. Can you see where those mistakes have been repeated?

_____
_____
_____
_____

What is happening in current events today? Where could we be potentially repeating history? Studying the past is only important if it ensures a better future. After all, history is past. It cannot be changed. We are living in the now. The future is determined by what we are doing now.

Today I will try to see patterns that have repeated. I will try to learn from history, so that I can help to see that mistakes will not be repeated.

Dear God,

Help me to see the mistakes that have been repeated throughout history. Help us to avoid repeating the mistakes of history and give us the courage and wisdom to change things we need to change.

Thank you, God!

November 18

MANIPULATING OTHERS

When we manipulate people, it means that we convince them to do something for our gain. For example, you convince your brother to share his candy with you even though you give him nothing in return. Or you stroke your friend's ego to convince him to do your homework for you because he is smarter than you.

There are times when you will bargain with another person. It is not manipulating when both sides benefit. When others are manipulated, they feel used. How do you feel when someone talks you into doing something you do not really want to do and from which you will not benefit? _____
_____
_____
_____
_____

Today I give up manipulating others. I will make sure everyone benefits (see Win-Win Strategies, p. 151).

Dear God,

Help me to see when I am manipulating someone else. Teach me methods by which everyone benefits.

Thank you, God!

November 19
PLEASING OTHERS

Many young people are "pleasers." They want to please everyone and be thought of as cooperative and helpful. These are very good traits to develop. There are times though when people will unintentionally take advantage of you if you try to please too much. You will notice this when you no longer enjoy doing whatever it is that they ask you to do. It is OK to ask them to ask someone else. Tell them you like doing whatever you are helping them with, but would they please spread the task around?

Learn to say "no" gracefully. "Thank you for asking me. I am not able to do it this time." "Please ask again another time." or "Can someone else take a turn now?"

Today I will learn to gracefully say "no" when I no longer enjoy what I am doing for someone else.

Dear God,

I want to contribute and to please others. But help me to know when I need to say "no" and to do so in a loving manner.

Thank you, God!

I need to say "no" to this person today: _____
about: _____

Here is what I will say: _____

November 20
TAKE A STROLL

On any given day, just as we are finishing school, we rush on to music lessons, dance lessons, sport activities, or language lessons. After supper, if we are lucky enough to eat with the family, there is homework or play practice, or some other activity. Whew! It seems like life is a whirlwind.

Plan a quiet walk. Notice that when you are walking, you are able to appreciate the trees, birds, squirrels, and nature in general. You are able to see people and wave or talk to them. You can be deep in thought and have conversations with yourself and with God. When you are driving by in a hurry to get somewhere, you miss all this. That is why walking is a good way to commune with God and to experience what is really happening around you.

Today I will take a walk and absorb the sights, sounds, and experiences that can only be had by walking.

Dear God,

In the rush to get somewhere we often miss what we pass by. Walking has its own rewards. Help me to rediscover them.

Thank you, God!

November 21
HOPE

Everyone needs to have hope of things getting better...of good things to come. Without it, life becomes meaningless and people fall into despair. This is where a spiritual outlook helps.

God can change the worst scenario into a positive one. God can change a wounded soul into a forgiving, accepting, and loving one. God provides us with hope of the goodness that is only God's to give. The little word "hope" has a tremendous impact on our lives. It gives us the courage to face our fears and to move forward toward a brighter end.

Today I give thanks for hope being alive in me. I will keep hope alive inside me.

Dear God,

Thank you for giving me hope in my future. When I do face the hard times in my life, keep that flame of hope burning within me so that I will be able to overcome.

Thank you, God!

Here are my hopes: _____
_____
_____
_____
_____

November 22
STRUCTURE OR NO STRUCTURE?

How well do you know yourself? How do you do your best? Do you like a structured day or an unstructured one? A structured day is one that is well-planned, with studies and activities happening according to an orderly schedule. An unstructured day is one in which you do whatever strikes you. Which helps you to be your best? Did you ever have an unplanned day off from school and feel lost?

Artists and creative people often favor unstructured days. They like to work when the ideas are flowing. That can sometimes be late at night. Others do well with a highly scheduled day. That is when they feel their most productive. Some people need to have someone telling them what to do all the time. Others are self-directed and do not need to be told what to do. They just anticipate what needs to be done and do it. Which one are you?

Today I will take a closer look at my habits. Do I like structure or lack of structure? If I am not sure, I will write about it in my journal.

Dear God,

Help me to get a clear picture of who I am and how I best operate. Help me to know myself better.

Thank you, God!

November 23

SEXUAL HARASSMENT

Sexual harassment is when someone uses words or behavior directed at a person because of his or her gender. These remarks which are uninvited, unwelcome, and inappropriate, cause the person on the receiving end to feel uncomfortable and offended.

Here are examples of sexual harassment:
- Snapping a girl's bra strap. Unwelcome touching is unacceptable.
- Jokes that point out sexual body parts.
- Remarks that make a member of the opposite sex feel diminished.
- Grabbing someone physically in a sexual area.

Sexual harassment needs to be stopped. If it happens to you, be sure to tell the offender you do not approve. If it continues, report it to your school authorities or another responsible adult. Sexual harassment shows disrespect for its victims. It should not be taken lightly. Do not support anyone who is participating in sexual harassment. Your silence condones and encourages their behavior.

Today I will guard my words and actions so they do not offend anyone.

Dear God,

I do not wish to take part in sexual harassment. Let my words and actions never offend.

Thank you, God!

Here is a time I witnessed sexual harassment and how I responded: _____

How will I respond next time? _____

November 24

DEALING WITH DIVORCE

Young people of divorced families often feel confused, sad, angry, rejected, and insecure. Some young children even believe the divorce happened because of something they did. This is not true. Divorce happens when the relationship between the parents fails to work any longer. Everyone is left feeling sad and confused. Many times the custodial parent and children have to find a new home and new school because financial circumstances change. Often the mother has to work full-time. New relationships may emerge. It is a time of change for everyone.

If your parents are getting divorced, you may be feeling unforgiving and angry. Remember to talk to God. Write in your journal about your feelings so you can better understand yourself and what you are going through. Many times young people feel that they do not get heard during this time. Write a letter to your parent(s) to explain your feelings and fears. Try not to take sides. Remember that both parents love you. Let them work out their disagreements. Do not get involved. Just let both of your parents know you love them. Pray for the best outcome to occur.

Today I will give consideration and empathy to anyone whose family is going through divorce. They may be needing my friendship, support, and good listening skills.

Dear God,

Sometimes relationships no longer work. Let me not judge but instead be supportive of anyone involved. I pray that the very best situation will occur for them.

Thank you, God!

Ways I can help myself or someone else in a divorce situation:
_____
_____

November 25

HEALING EARTH MEDITATION

Go into a quiet place. Take 20 or more deep breaths. Tell God that you wish to join all those meditating or praying for healing and transformation of earth.

Now envision earth in front of you. Imagine a violet flame surrounding the earth. Maybe it is like a pilot light at the bottom and when turned on high, a violet flame enfolds the earth, with darker purple flames licking the outer edges. Earth becomes a white ball inside the flames. You may see a swirling blue healing light come in and out around the earth.

If you have a word you wish to chant (peace, non-judgment, joy, unconditional love), do this now. Feel tremendous love in your heart for your home, planet earth. When you are finished, give thanks to God for the healing and transformation that is happening on your planet. Were there any messages for you? If so, you may wish to write in your journal what you received.

Today I know I am part of the healing and transformation going on in this planet. I will ask God what part I have in this healing.

Dear God,

Thank you for this beautiful earth and all the changes taking place on it. Help me to trust that you see the big picture. Let me not get lost in the small details.

Thank you, God!

Action: Write in your journal about the impressions and feelings you experienced in meditation.

November 26

*Today
I give thanks
for the Present,
in which destinies
can be changed.*

*Thank you,
God!*

November 27

SUPERSTITIONS

Superstitions such as "don't step on a crack or you will break your mother's back" or "a broken mirror is 7 years of bad luck" have been around for a long time. They have no power over you if you do not believe in them.

In many countries, superstitions still have an impact on people's lives. A Russian woman advised everyone not to talk across the threshold of their doorway because bad things could happen. A Malaysian exchange student said that many superstitions are part of their culture, but when she arrived here, she saw that we did not practice them and so she forgot all about them. They no longer had power over her. You choose—will superstitions have power over you?

Today I choose faith in my own power and my ability to decide how I wish to live my life.

Dear God,

Thank you for my power of choice. Clarify for me what is real and what is not.

Thank you, God!

Superstitions I do not believe: _____
_____
_____
_____
_____

November 28
THANKSGIVING

Thanksgiving is a time to reflect on the blessings you have received from God. It is a time to renew family and friend relationships. When the Pilgrims first arrived, they took time to give thanks for the harvest and to share it with the Native Americans. They were very grateful for new beginnings and the freedom to worship God as they pleased.

Today I will reflect on the many blessings God has given to me. I list some of them here.

_____
_____
_____
_____
_____
_____
_____
_____
_____
_____
_____
_____
_____
_____
_____
_____
_____

Dear God,

You have been so good to me. Help me to be more aware of all of the blessings you have given me.

Thank you, God!

November 29
DRUGS AND ALCOHOL

Drugs and alcohol numb the senses and take away inhibitions. When taken as prescribed they can have healing effects. As in everything, there is a balance and a responsibility. You will not want to put anything in your body that harms it. Many users are in denial and unconscious about how their misuse harms themselves and others. If you are not fully conscious, you may act in ways that harm yourself and others. Driving while under the influence of drugs or alcohol is one of them. Each year many people are injured or killed by drunk driving. Do not ride with anyone who has been drinking. Abuse of others also happens when under the influence of drugs and alcohol. Choose to trust your inner guide. Make a policy on how you will conduct your life and live by it.

Today I choose to live consciously in full celebration of life.

Dear God,

There are times when I am pressured to use drugs and alcohol. Give me strength to overcome and stick by my convictions. Thank you for the wonderful gift of experiencing life through my body.

Thank you, God!

Action: Look up the 12-Step Program for people who are addicted. See how the 12 steps help those people to overcome their addictions.

November 30
HANUKKAH

Hanukkah is a celebration of the victory of the few Jews over the many Greeks and the reclaiming and cleansing of the temple in 162 B.C. When the Jews entered the temple, they found only enough oil to light a candle for one night. Miraculously, it lasted for 8 days. For each of the 8 days of Hanukkah, the Jewish people light one candle. The menorah has nine candle holders. The Shamash, the tallest candle, is used to light the other candles.

During Hanukkah, Jews have festive meals and play dreidel games and other games. Then they light the candles and read the Torah and the Al hanissim prayer. A gift is given each night. It is a time of prayer and thanksgiving to God for allowing their culture, traditions, and beliefs to prevail.

Today I will give thanks to God for the freedom to worship as we choose.

Dear God,

I give thanks for the Jews and the richness they have added to our culture.

Thank you, God!

Action: Read about Hanukkah.

December 1
INTENTION FOR THE DAY

Live life with the purpose of being the best you can be. Choose an intention to concentrate on each day. For example, you might choose to love everyone unconditionally, meaning you will love them without judgment. Or perhaps you concentrate on trusting your inner voice. You choose what you wish to work on. At the end of the day reflect on how you did. Remember not to work on too many things at once or it will be difficult to remain focused. Have a "singleness of purpose." By writing in your journal you will be able to see your progress.

Today I will choose an intention for the day and reflect on it all day.

Dear God,

I am learning to see my spirit as a living, growing thing. As I am growing physically and mentally, I am also growing spiritually. Guide my efforts for my highest good.

Thank you, God!

My intention for the day is: _____
_____
_____

December 2
IMPOSING YOUR WILL

Many people feel that love gives them the right to impose their will on others. God loves everyone unconditionally and gives each of us freedom of choice. We have the freedom to make our own mistakes, to pay consequences, and to redirect our lives. This is the way God wants us to love each other...without judgment and without enforcing our will on each other.

When people you love are doing something for which they might have to pay a large consequence, pray for them. It is the most powerful thing you can do for them. Pray for your enemies as well. See them surrounded by love. When one knows the love of God and love of self, he or she can do nothing but love others with that same love.

Today I will not impose my will on anyone. I will seek out the love of God and myself so I can truly love others.

Dear God,

Make it clear when I am imposing my will on others. I know that you love me just as I am. Help me to love myself and others with such a love.

Thank you, God!

A way I may try to force my will on someone else is:
_____
_____
_____

I will change this behavior to: _____
_____
_____
_____

December 3
GOOD GROOMING

Good grooming makes you more appealing to others and promotes better health. Good grooming involves:
- Brushing your teeth at a minimum of two times daily
- Brushing or combing your hair several times daily and having your hair cut periodically
- Bathing or showering regularly and washing your hair
- Manicuring your fingernails and toenails
- Wearing clean clothes that fit correctly

As you enter your teen years, when body changes are taking place, you may wish to try some of the products available for body odor.

Good grooming makes you feel confident in yourself when interacting with others. Often, young people who do not feel good about themselves on the inside do not put forth much effort on the outside. Good grooming is a reflection of your overall well-being.

Today I will make sure I practice good grooming habits.

Dear God,

Good grooming is a reflection of how I feel about myself. I know you love me just as I am. Help me to see the inner spirit of all people I meet today and love them as they are.

Thank you, God!

The good grooming habits I will practice are:
_____
_____

This is how I feel about myself: _____
_____
_____

December 4
SOCIAL POISE

What is social poise? Have you met people who seemed to be comfortable with themselves and at ease in any situation? People with social poise knows how to make others comfortable. They accept others as they come, without excessive expectations.

It is important to study manners and customs so that you know how to act, but even more important is to be able to make the other person feel comfortable and accepted. When you are around others who are judging you on whether your house measures up or if your manners are by the book, you feel uncomfortable, and that's how others will feel if you do that to them.

Another element worth noting is your ability to communicate. This means being able to make conversation that focuses on others rather than on yourself. Good communication also involves being able to follow through with commitments. If you say you will go somewhere, show up or call in advance to say why you cannot be there. Many books have been written on conduct. Study them, but also trust your inner self to act in a way that makes others feel comfortable and accepted around you.

Today I will study codes of conduct and be mindful of making others feel comfortable.

Dear God,

You always love me as I am. Help me to make others feel comfortable around me. Let my behavior and words not offend.

Thank you, God!

Manners and customs that make me feel comfortable:

_____
_____

December 5
PREPARATION FOR CHRISTMAS

Christmas involves the hustle and bustle of shopping for the perfect gifts for family and friends. It is the smell of favorite foods prepared in celebration and the sight of beautiful decorations signifying family traditions. It is the sound of melodious carols being sung for others. Christmas is a time of great peace and joy.

For some it can be a time of feeling lonely or feeling the loss of someone dear. It can be a time of tension when finances are tight.

Christmas does not need to be about "things." It is about sharing love. Think about a gift that expresses your desire to share yourself. Perhaps you can build something, make a craft, bake something, write a poem or song, or give of your time in some way that pleases another. A gift you make is a true gift of the heart. Be sure to think of the less fortunate, too, or invite someone to join in who will otherwise be alone.

Today I will ask God for gift ideas that will be the best expression of myself and my love.

Dear God,

I wish to give joy to those I love. Help me to give a gift of the heart designed just for each one. Also, help me to be a good receiver of gifts, too.

Thank you, God!

December 6
GET THE RIGHT START

The purpose of childhood and the teenage years is to give you time to prepare for adulthood, when actions are less forgiving and accountability is demanded. Parents and teachers do their best to make you ready. Often, young people are unaware of what they need to be successful. Once you are an adult, there will be a gradual shift from being the student to eventually being the teacher. With the freedoms of adulthood come responsibilities. You will be expected to be self-sufficient, meaning that you support yourself and start contributing to the community to which you belong.

Adults must have a means to support themselves. Training will be necessary. The more training you have, the more flexibility you will have in determining how and where you will work and live. It is important to prepare for how to support yourself while you are still single and not having to support others as well. What you think you will be doing may not be what you will be doing over your lifetime, but that does not matter. What matters is that you give yourself a good start. You can always add to your training and will actually be guided to do so later on in your life.

Today I wish to give myself a good start. I will make plans for my training and get guidance from God, my parents, and others.

Dear God,

Guide my plans to give me a good start. Keep me focused until I am well on my way. Thank you for your love and caring.

Thank you, God!

The kind of training I think I need is: _____

_____

December 7

*Today I give thanks
for the peace
and joy of the
holiday season.*

Thank you, God!

December 8
FOCUS YOUR ENERGY

Your body is made of energy. You use that energy in school for thinking, during recess, and for singing. You use it when you play sports, do chores, or take music lessons. You restore your energy when you eat, rest, get sunshine, and exercise. Many times, energy gets too scattered. You try to do too many things, afraid that you might miss out on something.

Focus your energy. This means that in order to be very good at something, you must concentrate your energy on the thing you want to do. If it is karate, focus on karate and let go of some other activities. Otherwise, your energy goes to too many places, and you will not be good at anything. Another example is club memberships. You can belong to several clubs and just be a member, or you can belong to one club and be actively involved. It is your choice. Remember that you get more out of the experiences in which you participate. It takes more energy to get out of trouble than to stay out of trouble. It takes more energy to frown than to smile.

Today I will think about where my energy goes. Am I managing my energy effectively, or do I need to make changes?

Dear God,

Help me to take care of my energy system. I want to be effective in how I use my energy. Let me know how to make good choices.

Thank you, God!

I am focusing my energy on: _____
_____
_____

December 9
HOLIDAYS ARE NOT ABOUT RECEIVING

Some people get depressed during the holiday season. They feel they cannot share the joy of the season because they are too poor, or there is no one with whom to share it, or it is too commercial, and so on. There are many reasons why people do not get into the spirit. The holidays are not about what you receive; they are about what you give of yourself. Find ways to help others during the holidays. If you do not have much money, give gifts of time, such as baking, car washes, yard work, house cleaning, and so on. The holidays can become commercial if you allow them to be. The holiday spirit is a matter of the heart and mind. A person with the spirit reflects love, joy, and peacefulness. You can do this on a daily basis.

Today I will reflect the holiday spirit—love, joy, and peace.

Dear God,

If I get sad about my situation during the holidays, help me to see some positive alternatives. Help me to see that love, joy, and peace are qualities I can have every day.

Thank you, God!

Gifts of time I can give today are: _____
_____
_____
_____
_____

December 10
GIVING GIFTS

Joy is found in the giving of gifts. Choosing a special gift tailored to a specific person requires imagination and thought. To make it a gift from the heart, add a poem or letter of appreciation. Think of a gift the person would like, not just what you would like to have. If you are giving to a brother or sister, you might offer to do his or her chores for a specified length of time. Giving unexpected hugs, praise, kindness, or smiles will brighten anyone's day. These are truly gifts of the heart. At gift-giving times, consider something special from both your heart and your pocketbook or use your creativity to make the gift. These will be gifts long remembered.

Today I will give gifts that require more of me than just spending money. I will give gifts from the heart.

Dear God,

Help me to show the honor and appreciation I feel each time I give a gift to someone. Guide me to give creative gifts from the heart.

Thank you, God!

Gifts from the heart I will give are: _____

December 11
MIRACLES

Miracles happen in everyday lives to those who are open to them. If you are not open to miracles, one may happen, but you may not recognize it.

Sometimes a person may pray for a miracle to happen to change the course of some situation. If the person prayed for a specific action to happen, such as for his or her team to win a game, it may not happen because it is not the best solution for all involved. God knows the bigger picture. The prayer should always be for the highest good for everyone involved, or in this case, for the person and his or her team to play their best. Pray and then let go of the outcome.

God loves to perform miracles when they are least expected. God does not like to give miracles simply to prove to someone that God exists. Let go of expectation. Allow the miracles to come. Be open to them.

Today I am open to miracles in my life.

Dear God,

Thank you for miracles in my life and in the world around me.

Thank you, God!

Miracles I have seen, experienced, or heard about:
_____
_____
_____
_____

December 12
IN TIMES OF CRISIS

In times of crisis, events always seem worse than they really are. Take a walk, do a workout, meditate or just sleep on it, or talk to a friend. The next day you will have a fresher outlook. Remember to talk to God about it. Turn over those things you do not feel capable of handling alone. God has a way of making miracles happen. Believe that God will do just that for you.

Time can heal many things. Remember to give it time. We cannot run away from our problems, even though we often wish we could. However, getting a change of scenery can sometimes give you a new perspective. Maybe a sleepover at a friend's house or a few nights of camping will help.

Today I will think of how I will handle crises. What could I do better the next time to make the outcome more positive?

_____
_____
_____
_____

Dear God,

You are my partner. Help me to remember to call on you in times of crisis.

Thank you, God!

December 13

I am as God created me.
I live this day in
pure love, joy, and peace.
I see only truth.
I forgive everyone
and myself of any
perceived
wrongs.

Thank you,
God!

December 14

THE VALUE OF MONEY

Money is a tool that is used to buy things that we need or want. Money can be used for good or for evil. Money itself is not evil. How it is used will determine its value.

Money is a tool. It buys "things," but it cannot buy love, happiness, joy, or peace. Some of the richest people are the most miserable. How you manage your money will determine the success of your life. Will you spend it on yourself? Will you help others in need? Will you hoard it in a bank? Will you spend it on items for which you lose interest in a short time, or will you invest it in items that have longer-term benefit.

Today I will look at how I am spending my money. Do my spending habits reflect my beliefs about money? Am I good at doing things with my money? I will write about this in my journal.

Dear God,

I need your guidance in spending my money. Thank you for the money that you have given to me. Let me not be greedy with my resources. Instead guide me in making wise decisions and sharing my gifts with others.

Thank you, God!

This is what I have spent my money on in the last two weeks:
_____
_____

Is it in line with what I consider important? _____
_____

Have I shared my resources? _____
_____

December 15
LETTING GO OF ENVY

Envy is what you feel when you wish you had something that belongs to another. For example, perhaps you feel your sister or brother gets all of your mom and dad's attention, or your best friend has better clothes than you.

Envy is a feeling that robs you of the ability to appreciate what you do have. Ask God to release the envy you have. Write down all of the good things you have for which you should be grateful.

Today I will be grateful for all of the blessings God has given me.

Dear God,

When I am feeling envious of someone for something I wish I could have, help me count my blessings instead. If I want it bad enough, I will set positive goals for getting what I want. I know you will not deny me what is best for me.

Thank you, God!

I am grateful for these blessings: _____
_____
_____
_____

December 16
HAVING TO PROVE YOURSELF

There may be times while you are young when a remark made by an unthinking adult makes you feel inferior. Or maybe a situation causes you to be at a disadvantage, and you say to yourself, "When I grow up, I will never let this happen again." or "I will prove to them that I am not a loser!" From that point on, you make choices and channel your energy to prove to yourself and others that they were wrong or that you are more than they thought you were. Focusing on proving yourself to others puts them in charge of your life. Ask yourself whether you are really wanting to prove something to them or to yourself.

Proving yourself can be good if you achieve your goal. However, if you take another's remark as your own, you may develop a deep-seated low opinion of yourself that never allows you to enjoy your successes once you reach them. You may get stuck on the obsessive behavior of proving yourself. Ask yourself, "Was this remark true or valid?" "If not, when will I have reached my goal?" "When will I stop needing to prove myself?"

Today I will examine my life for ways I think I need to prove myself and see if they are valid.

Dear God,

I know that you love me just as I am right now. Help me to know that love deep inside.

Thank you, God!

Ways I may be feeling I need to prove something about myself:
_____
_____

When I will know I have proven myself: _____
_____

December 17
BLOOD THICKER THAN WATER?

You may hear statements such as, "He's a chip off the old block." or "Those Johnsons are all alike." Families share many close experiences together—both struggles and good times. You learn much from your family. You inherit genetic tendencies and physical attributes. Your environment can also influence your upbringing and who you turn out to be.

However, you are your own person. How you react to your life experiences is up to you. In today's world of single parent families, job mobility, and untraditional families, you may find deep friendship and nurturing through close neighbors and friends. They may actually be closer than family and in some cases more reliable. Family is being redefined in today's society. You may need to look for nurturing relationships wherever you can find them. That's OK. Just trust God to take care of you. Call on God when you need help and when you just want to talk.

Today I will look for the lessons I am learning with my family, neighbors, and friends.

Dear God,
We are all in your family. Help me to develop the nurturing relationships I need to grow into the caring, loving adult you want me to be.

Thank you, God!

Traits I am glad I inherited or acquired: _____
_____
_____
_____

December 18
FIND YOUR CREATIVE SELF

Each person God creates has some creativity. Some people discover it through drawing and painting. Others discover musical talents. Some people find their creativity through their work, cooking, how they dress, writing, building things, and so on. Finding your creative self brings joy. Have you ever noticed how you can lose all sense of time when you are doing something creative? You completely lose yourself in it. Ask yourself, "What do I do that brings forth my creative self?" Do you put down potential creative ideas with statements such as, "That's silly" or "I'm not good at that"? Allow yourself free rein to be silly or even to do poorly at something. There may be a creative genius lurking just below the surface. Try new things, even if you fear you may not be any good. You may surprise yourself!

Today I will give my creative self a chance to be free to explore without judgment.

Dear God,

Thank you for talents yet undiscovered. Help me to find my own creative self and to unleash the joy I receive from doing so.

Thank you, God!

Ways I allow myself freedom to "just be me": _____
_____
_____
_____
_____

December 19

"I AM" EXERCISE

One way to know yourself better is to do the "I am" exercise. It is a fun thing to do in a group of friends or family. One person starts by saying, "I am _____" and gives a quality that he or she thinks is true, such as "I am peaceful." Then the next person says an "I am" statement pertaining to himself or herself and so on until everyone has had a turn. You can say as many different qualities that describe you as you wish, and it does not have to be done in any sort of order.

Other qualities you might think of include: I am...

funny	loving	loyal
hopeful	kind	joyful
trusting	truthful	faithful
forgiving	friendly	a good listener
thoughtful		

End with "Thank you, God."

Today I will focus on my good qualities.

Dear God,

What I think of myself is more important than what others think of me. Help me to know myself. Let me see myself as you see me.

Thank you, God!

Qualities I believe are true about myself:
_____
_____
_____
_____

December 20
BEING GRATEFUL

We are given many gifts every day by God that we fail to notice. We have food to eat, shelter over our heads, parents to watch over us, clothes to keep us warm, and so on. In addition, many things are free to us—blue skies with billowy clouds, fresh air, flowers, shrubs, trees, green grass, the smile of a friend, and laughter.

Develop a habit of taking note of those things we often take for granted. Pretty soon you will find it easier to be pleased and happy. Give thanks to God often and abundantly. God will bless you even more.

Today I will take note of the many "free" things that add to my happiness every day. I will give thanks to God for:

_____
_____
_____
_____
_____

Dear God,

You are so generous in your giving to me. Thank you. Please help me to take more notice of the things you offer so abundantly. Develop in me a grateful heart.

Thank you, God!

December 21

WINTER SOLSTICE: TIME FOR QUIET REFLECTION

Winter is the time of year when outdoor activity often slows because of less sun and more inclement weather. It is an ebb time for us. We need to take time for quiet reflection.

Deliberately slow down so you can be more conscious of what is going on around you. Take time for games played with family members or do a puzzle. Write down your thoughts. Take a hot bath. Join others in a brisk walk, go sledding, read a book, feed the wild animals. Spend time with those who are important to you.

Today I will just be. If something strikes me, I will do it...otherwise, I will just enjoy the quiet.

Dear God,

It is OK to have a slower time. Help me to live my life consciously. Thank you for my family and friends. Thank you for just allowing me to "be."

Thank you, God!

What I learned from my quiet time today: _____
_____
_____
_____
_____
_____
_____
_____

December 22
LOOKING FOR EVIDENCE OF GOOD

You need only to turn on the evening news or read the daily paper to think that everything is wrong with the world. That is the illusion! The truth is that there is much good happening. If you have been studying history lately, you see that we have progressed significantly in our thinking and we are continuing to do so. From cave man to medieval times...to the wars...and now to high technology. We are awakening to our own humanity. Because communication through technology has brought the parts of the world so much closer to each other, we are able to discern truth without it being suppressed by the powers in place. The truth will set us free.

Look again at your newspapers and other news sources. Look past the sensational news stories to those movements and trends that have a real impact on you and your community. See the individuals who are working to make a difference. Check legislation being passed that makes a difference in people's lives. If your intention is to look for the good, you will find more than you thought was possible. This is the hope about which Jesus spoke. Keep an attitude of hope.

Today I will look for the good happening right now in my world. I will maintain an attitude of hope.

Dear God,

Thank you for holding the vision for us even when we forget. Help us to trust in your guidance and give us hope of the good things to come.

Thank you, God!

Here is the good I discovered happening in my world today:
_____
_____
_____

December 23
NEGOTIATION

To negotiate means that two parties from two differing viewpoints patiently talk to one another in an effort to achieve a common goal. Negotiation requires a willingness to understand the other party and the other party's needs. It requires patience and a willingness to compromise in order to reach a specific goal. Sometimes when two parties have very differing viewpoints, a mediator or neutral party is brought in to hear both sides. Not being attached to either viewpoint, the mediator attempts to help each side understand the other's viewpoints and needs so a fair outcome can be obtained.

As you can see, negotiating is a sophisticated and sometimes lengthy process, but the outcome can be worthwhile. Examples of negotiating are peace efforts in Northern Ireland and the Middle East. As you get older, you may be called upon to use negotiating skills in your life.

Today I will work on developing skills of listening to other viewpoints and determining the needs of other people—patience and a willingness to compromise.

Dear God,

Teach me skills to help bring people together toward peace filled goals.

Thank you, God!

I can use negotiating skills today by: _____
_____
_____
_____
_____

December 24

CHOOSING TO BE AT PEACE

What do you think of when you choose to be at peace? What makes you feel peaceful? Is it a beautiful meadow with blue skies and clouds? Or being at a lake or at the ocean listening to the sound of waves crashing and gulls screeching? Flying a kite or a picnic at the park? Sometimes music makes us feel at peace.

Peace is a state of well-being when we are feeling quiet and emotionally well. Peace is a state of being that we can choose.

Instead of choosing to fight, we can choose to either change our attitude or compromise. Instead of choosing to feel sad, we can think of things that make us happy. This is not to say that you will never again experience sadness or anger and wanting to fight, but it does mean that you have a choice on how you will respond. A peaceful response is one of your choices.

Today I will observe when I am feeling peaceful and when I am not at peace. Then I will change thoughts, attitudes, or actions to bring me to peace again.

Dear God,

Help me to recognize when I am not at peace and to change my behavior or thoughts to be peaceful. When I change myself to be more peaceful, I will influence others around me to be more peaceful. Help me to make it so.

Thank you, God!

Here's what being at peace means to me: _____
_____
_____
_____

December 25
CHRISTMAS DAY

Prepare for a Christmas of the heart. Write a letter to each person in your family and your friends. Tell them what you appreciate about them and what they mean to you. Jesus modeled unconditional love and forgiveness during his stay on earth. This day is a celebration of his existence. If there is anyone against whom you have been holding anger or a grudge, take this opportunity to ask Jesus for help to let it go. Pray for forgiveness and pray for the world, that peace, love, and joy will prevail.

Christmas is a time when minds come together in love, peace, and harmony. Express your gratitude to God for all the good that has been brought into your life.

Today I love everyone. I forgive everyone and myself and am grateful for all my blessings. I will model peace and joy for others.

Dear God,

You have given me much for which to be grateful. I pray for peace, harmony, and love to prevail over the earth. May this spirit of love continue into the new year.

Thank you, God!

December 26
KWANZAA

Kwanzaa is a spiritual celebration for African Americans that began in 1966. The purpose was to bring black people together to acknowledge their cultural contributions, unify and support black families, and promote the oneness and goodness of life. It has no ties to religion and takes place from December 26th to December 31st. Kwanzaa is based on seven principles that govern conduct.

Unity   To strive and maintain unity of family, community, and nation and as a race.
Self-determination   To define, name, create, and speak for ourselves.
Collective work and responsibility   To promote community caring and effort.
Cooperative economics   To encourage African Americans in business and support their success.
Purpose   To build and develop our community and restore its greatness.
Creativity   To do as much as we can, in the way we can, to leave our community more beautiful and beneficial than when we inherited it.
Faith   To believe with all our hearts in our parents, teachers, and leaders and our people and in the righteousness and victory of our struggle.

Today I honor all people and their contributions to our society.

Dear God,

**Thank you for the contributions of all people.
We are all one.**

Thank you, God!

Action: I will research a person who has made contributions for the benefit of all of us.

December 27

*Today I am seeing myself
as Whole and Perfect,
a Child of God made
in God's image.*

*Thank you,
God!*

December 28

MOTIVATION

When a person is motivated, he or she feels prompted to act on an idea. Heart and mind are joined in agreement on the idea, and this induces action. There may be a time that you are asked to do something such as clean your room or write an essay. You may not feel motivated. It was not your idea. However, if you have a friend coming over to spend the night, you might be motivated to clean your room without anyone even asking you to do so. If the topic of the essay is one you choose and in which you have interest, you might be very motivated to write it. You will benefit by learning more about the topic and then in sharing your interest with others who read your story.

Understanding motivation is an important part of knowing yourself and others. What motivates you to action? Write in your journal about this. Observe when others become motivated.

Today I will observe what motivates me and others and write about it in my journal.

Dear God,

Finding motivation is difficult at times. Help me to understand what motivates me and others and how to use motivation in my life.

Thank you, God!

December 29
SOCIALIZING

Making friends usually involves experiences shared over a period of time. When you are being social, you open yourself up for experiences with others. Sometimes, you will have to make the first move in planning an event and inviting others to it. You may have to introduce yourself to people you do not know. Do not be afraid! They are just as uncomfortable as you are. They, too, are concerned that you might not like them or have anything in common with them. Some simple social situations you might consider inviting others to are:
- Going out for ice cream or a soda
- Riding bikes and having a picnic in the park
- Seeing a movie
- Coming to your home to play games, cards, pool, and so on
- Going to a school event

If you do not hit it off after the first or second time with someone, continue socializing elsewhere but always agree to be friends. Socializing provides a means to meet new people and have fun while doing it.

Today I will make the effort to socialize with someone I do not know very well by planning an event and inviting the person.

Dear God,

Thank you for the pleasurable ways we can get to know others. Give me courage to make the first move, if necessary, to get to know others. It will enrich my life even more.

Thank you, God!

Today I will invite (name) _____ to (activity)
_____

December 30

GENEROSITY

When people give of their talents and resources generously, it means they give unselfishly and abundantly. People who give generously often believe in noble causes that benefit others. In their heart and mind, they believe they are helping others and are very motivated to do so.

Philanthropists are people who have a great love of mankind. They aspire to projects that help others and try to develop projects that are beneficial to people. They are often very generous in giving of themselves and their resources. These people usually have a high-minded character. They hold a vision of what humanity can be and then do what they can to help it get there. They are often people of high integrity.

Today I will look at the ways I am able to be generous. I will seek to grow in generosity.

Dear God,

Help me to hold the vision of how good we can all be. Help me to be generous in giving of myself and my resources to others.

Thank you, God!

Ways I am generous: _____
_____
_____
_____

December 31
DANCE

In Lee Ann Womack's song, *I Hope You Dance,* she sings, "And when you get the choice to sit it out or dance, I hope you dance." This song is about choosing life. . . not doing what is safe but pushing yourself to experience new growth; establish new boundaries and horizons.

When you've been at a dance, have you chosen to sit along the sidelines, afraid that everyone will be looking at you? You probably ended up feeling left out of the fun, being bored and not having a good time. Getting past your fear to dance and letting yourself flow to the music is similar to what you will need to do with everything else in life. Take one step at a time. Let go of any fears of failure and lose yourself in the effort. DANCE!

Today I will acknowledge when I am feeling fear and ask God to help me let myself go so I can choose to live life fully.

Dear God,

Help me to get past the fears that block me from living life fully. Help me to experience the joy of living and learning.

Thank you, God!

List a time when you choose not to live life fully because you were afraid. How did you feel?

_____

_____

List a time when you chose to go for something with all your heart. How did it feel?

_____

_____

Summary Lesson
DOING A YEAR-END EVALUATION

The end of the year is a great time to review what you have done in the past year. What new skills did you learn? Did you belong to any clubs? Did you perform any works of charity? What kind of relationships do you have in your life? How would you like to change them?

What kind of relationship do you have with God? How would you like to change that?

Write below what you have accomplished:

_____
_____
_____
_____
_____
_____
_____
_____
_____
_____
_____

Today I reflect on what I have done or learned in the past year.

Dear God,

I wish to turn my weaknesses into strengths. Help me to see clearly where I might improve. I know I am right where I need to be now.

Thank you, God!

Photos

(New friends and family)

REFERENCES

1. Weston, Walter L. *The Self Healing Pocket Guide.* Ohio: Transitions Press. 1996.

2. Tiller, William A, PhD. *Science and Human Transformation.* California: Pavior Publishing. 1997.

3. Kirkwood, Annie, and Kirkwood, Byron. *Messages to Our Family.* Nevada: Blue Dolphin Publishing, Inc. 1994.

4. Reprinted from *Black Elk Speaks* by John G. Neihardt, by permission of the University of Nebraska Press. Copyright ©1932, 1959, 1972, by John G. Neihardt. Copyright ©1961 by the John G. Neihardt Trust.

5. Courtesy of Joel Arthur Barker, Founder and President, Infinity, Limited., an International Consulting Firm, New York, NY, 2001.

6. Rosenberg, Marshall B. *Nonviolent Communication: A Language of Compassion.* Texas: PuddleDancer Press. 1996.

BIBLIOGRAPHY

Canfield, Jack, Hansen, Mark Victor, and Kirberger, Kimberly. *Chicken Soup for the Teenage Soul.* Florida: Health Communications, Inc. 1997.

Covey, Sean. *The 7 Habits of Highly Effective Teens.* New York: Fireside, a division of Simon & Schuster. 1998.

Ford, Judy. *Wonderful Ways to Love a Teen . . . Even When It Seems Impossible.* California: Conari Press, distributed by Publishers Group West. 1996.

Helmering, Doris Wild. *Sense Ability.* New York: Eagle Brook, an imprint of William Morrow and Company, Inc. 1999.

Lindesell, Harold. *Harper Study Bible: The Holy Bible.* Michigan: Zondervan Bible Publishers. 1962.

McMahon, Tom. *Teen Tips: A Practical Survival Guide for Parents with Kids 11 to 19.* New York: Pocket Books, a division of Simon & Schuster, Inc. 1996.

Wilmes, David J. *Parenting for Prevention.* Minnesota: Johnson Institute Books. 1988.

INDEX

A

Abuse, 309
Acceptance, 285
Accepting Consequences, 175
Accepting Constructive Criticism, 174
Accepting My Body, 63
Accepting My Good, 157
Accepting Myself, 64
Accepting Others, 40
Accountable, Being, 197
Acting With Dignity, 103
Addictions, Eliminating, 163
Addressing Seniors With Respect, 84
Advice, Giving, 203
All Saints' Day, 263
Angels, 147
Anger, Handling, 184
Anger, Letting Go of, 11
Appearances, Keeping Up, 310
Appreciating Myself, 190
Appreciation, Showing, 44
April Fool's Day, 91
Arrogance, 241
Asking for Guidance, 80
Attitude Is Everything, 108

B

Back to School, 230
Bad Day, Everyone Has a, 152
Bad Day, Having a, 133
Balance Between Spirit, Mind, and Body, The 181
Balance, Finding, 192
Balance, Seeking, 212
Be Alive! 193
Be Happy! 176
Be With a Friend, 34
Beauty is Skin Deep, 302
Being a Good Loser, 183
Being a Good Sport, 74
Being a Good Winner, 182
Being a Team Player, 68
Being Accountable, 197
Being at Peace, 4
Being at Peace in Nature, 33
Being Aware, 111
Being Critical and Judgmental, 180
Being Discriminating, 25
Being Fully There for Others, 137
Being Open to New People, 274
Being on the Path, 10
Being Shy, 262
Being Still to Hear God's Voice, 30
Black and White Versus Gray Thinking, 313
Blaming Yourself or Others, 110
Blood Thicker Than Water? 351
Body, Accepting My, 63
Body, Listen to Your, 158
Boredom, 98
Boundaries, Setting, 255
Bragging or Boasting, 308
Breathe, 165
Brick Wall, Walking into, 221
Brighten the Corner Where You Are, 173
Bring Out the Best in Others, 143
Bringing Joy to Others, 23
Build Your House on a Strong Foundation: The Golden Rule, 121
Building Trust, 24
Building Versus Burning Bridges, 282
Burning the Candle at Both Ends, 288

370

C

Calling Names, Making Fun of Others of, 19
Care of Your Belongings, 100
Caught Being Bad, 92
Celebrating the 4th of July, 185
Celebrating Yourself, 9
Change, Dealing With, 272
Charitable Acts From Your Heart, Doing, 154
Cheating, 273
Choices to be Healthy, 124
Choices, Making, 8
Choosing To Be a Friend, 66
Choosing Friends, 216
Choosing To Be at Peace, 358
Chores, Doing, 95
Christmas Day, 359
Circle of Life, 215
Color in Your Life, Using, 319
Commitment, 226
Common Sense, Developing, 227
Communicating, 85
Communicating Feelings, 295
Community, Finding My Worth in, 113
Comparisons, 258
Competition, 129
Complaining, Whining and, 207
Conflict, Handling, 153
Confused, Feeling, 142
Consequences, Accepting, 175
Constructive Criticism, Accepting, 174
Conversing With Others, 257
Counting Our Blessings, 82
Courage, 117
Create Your Own Destiny, 278
Creative Inspiration, Needing, 284
Creative Self, Find Your, 352
Creativity: Declare It Good, 122
Crisis, In Times of, 346
Critical or Judgmental, Being, 180
Cynical or Critical, Being, 254

D

Dance, 365
Dead Right, 290
Dealing With Change, 272
Dealing With Illness, 65
Dealing With Walls People Construct Around Themselves, 146
Death, Dealing With, 32
Determining Strengths and Weaknesses, 71
Developing Common Sense, 227
Difference, Making a, 58
Difference One Person Can Make, What a, 29
Difficult Relationships, 291
Dignity, Acting With, 103
Disabilities, 260
Disappointed Someone, Today I Feel I, 37
Disappointment, Handling, 298
Discriminating, Being, 25
Discrimination, 188
Diversity, Respecting, 155
Divine Order, 2
Divorce, Dealing With, 328
Doing Charitable Acts, 154
Dreams, 307
Drugs and Alcohol, 333

E

Earth and Nature, Honoring, 112
Earth, Healing Meditation, 329
Easter, The Promise of, 90
Eating the Right Foods, 31
Eliminating Addictions, 163
Eliminating Violence, 109
End May Not Justify the Means, The, 305

Energy, Focus Your, 342
Envy, Letting Go of, 349
Every Day Is a New
    Beginning, 169
Everyone Has a Bad Day, 152
Evidence of Good, Looking
    for, 356
Excellence Versus Perfection, 118
Extremes, Going to, 89

F

Failure, 138
Faith, 167
Family Members, Treatment
    of, 267
Fathers, Honoring, 172
Fear, 128
Fear of Success, 107
Fear, Release of, 235
Feeling Confused, 142
Feeling Good About Yourself
    Without Putting Others
    Down, 97
Feeling Inferior, 78
Feeling Secure, 81
Feeling Sorry for Yourself, 206
Feeling Unworthy or Fear of
    Success, 107
Feelings, Communicating, 295
Fighting, 41
Fights, Picking, 22
Find Your Creative Self, 352
Finding Balance, 192
Finding the Joy, 127
Finding My Worth in My
    Community, 113
Finding Out Who We Are, 50
First Impressions, 202
Focus Your Energy, 342
Following Through, 277
Forgiveness of Oneself and
    Others, 16
Forgiving Parents, 161

Forgiving Yourself, 160
Foul Language, 164
Foundation, Build Your House on
    Strong, 121
Friend, Choosing To Be, 66
Friends, Money Does Not
    Buy, 279
Friends, The Importance of, 139

G

Generosity, 364
Get the Right Start, 340
Getting Someone Else in
    Trouble, 214
Giver or Taker? 294
Giving Advice, 203
Giving Gifts, 344
Giving of Oneself, 7
Giving Your Power Away, 125
Goals, New Year's, 1
Goals, Setting, 55
God Loves Children, 286
God Loves You as You Are Right
    Now, 292
Going to Extremes, 89
Golden Rule, 121
Good Decision, When Am I
    Making a, 99
Good Grooming, 337
Good, Looking for, 94
Good Loser, Being a, 183
Good Sport, Being a, 74
Good Winner, Being a, 182
Gossiping, 14
Grandparents, 251
Grass Is Not Always Greener,
    The, 162
Grateful, Being, 354
Greed and Selfishness, 238
Group Power, 120
Growing in Responsibility, 269
Growing Things, 194
Guidance, Asking for, 80

Guided, You Are Being, 244
Guilt, 275

H

Halloween, 304
Handling Anger, 184
Handling Conflict, 153
Handling Disappointment, 298
Handling Stress, 119
Hanukkah, 334
Happiness, 148
Happy! Be, 176
Harvest Time, 265
Having a Bad Day, 133
Having to Prove Yourself, 350
Healing Earth Meditation, 329
Healing Yourself, 150
Holidays Are Not About
    Receiving, 343
Honoring Earth and Nature, 112
Honoring Fathers, 172
Honoring Leaders of All
    Cultures, 48
Honoring Mothers, 130
Honoring People of All
    Colors, 21
Honoring People of All
    Occupations, 245
Honoring People of All Religions
    and Cultures, 297
Honoring People Who Have Died
    for Freedom, 149
Honoring St. Patrick, 76
Honoring Yourself and Others, 18
Hope, 325
Humor/Laughter, 145
Hurt Feelings, 61

I

"I AM" Exercise, 353
I Am Tired of School, 46
I Can't Change, 208

I Feel Like I Disappointed
    Someone Today, 37
Illness, Dealing with, 65
Importance of Friends, 139
Imposing Your Will, 336
Impulsiveness, 259
Inner Guide, Listen to, 240
Inner Power, Owning Your, 59
Integrity of Actions, 316
Intention for the Day, 335

J

Jealousy, Letting Go of, 13
Jesus' Trials and Forgiveness, 88
Journal, Keeping a, 312
Joy, 5
Joy, Bringing to Others, 23
Joy, Finding, 127
Judgment, 224

K

Keeping a Journal, 312
Keeping Up Appearances, 310
Keeping Our Perspective, 47
Kwanzaa, 360

L

Labels, 270
Lack or Plenty, 222
Language, Foul, 164
Laughter, Humor, 145
Leadership, The Meaning of, 49
Learning From Nature, 213
Learning From the Process, 209
Less is More, 42
Let Go of the Outcome, 234
Letting Go, 54
Letting Go of Anger, 11
Letting Go of Envy, 349
Letting Go of Jealousy, 13
Letting Your Light Shine, 17
Lies, Telling, 131
Life's Ebb and Flow, 134

Limiting Yourself, 289
Listen to Your Body, 158
Listen to Your Inner Guide, 240
Listen to Your Self-Talk, 159
Listening to Others, 303
Live Life in Moderation, 317
Living in the Present Moment, 57
Look for the Deeper Lesson, 236
Looking for Evidence of Good, 356
Looking for the Good in Everything, 94
Looking for the Good in Others, 69
Losing a Pet, 201
Love One Another as I Have Loved You, 3
Love Relationships, 243
Loyalty, 67

M

Making Choices, 8
Making a Difference, 58
Making Fun of Others or Calling Names, 19
Manipulating Others, 322
Manners, Using, 83
Meaning of Leadership, 49
Mistakes, Pointing Out, 189
Miracles, 345
Models, Role, 38
Modeling Jesus' Life, 191
Moderation, Live Life in, 217
Money Does Not Buy Friends, 279
Money, The Value of, 348
Monitoring TV and Advertising, 106
Mood Affects Others, Your, 268
Mothers, Honoring, 130
Motivation, 362
Mountains Versus Mole Hills, 318
Move Too Quickly, Trying to, 252

N

Nature, Learning From, 213
Need Versus Want, 229
Needing Creative Inspiration, 284
Negative Feelings and Thinking, 52
Negotiation, 357
Never Say "Never," 186
New Beginnings Every Day, 169
New Is Not Always Better, 179
New Year's Goals, 1

O

Oneness, Recognizing Our, 132
Open Yourself to Others, 247
Our Efforts Make a Difference, 281
Outer Exploration, 43
Overwhelming, When Things Seem, 36
Ownership, 301
Owning a Pet, 170
Owning Your Inner Power, 59

P

Passover, 87
Patience, 51
Peace, Being at, 4
Peace, Choosing, 358
Peace in Nature, 33
Perfection, Excellence Versus, 118
Perseverance, 116
Perspective, Keeping Our, 47
Pet, Losing a, 201
Pet, Owning a, 170
Picking Fights, 22
Playing Sports, 141
Pleasing Others, 323
Pointing Out Mistakes, 189
Positive Thinking, 53
Possibilities, Unlimited, 239
Power, Giving Away, 125

Power of Prayer, 60
Power of Thoughts, 223
Prayer, Serenity, 231
Praying, 177
Praying With Your Family, 249
Preparation for Christmas, 339
Preparing for Summer
  Vacation, 135
Present Moment, Living in, 57
Pride, 248
Problem, Whose Is It?, 287
Procrastinating, 300
Protection, 95
Prove Yourself, Having to, 350
Putting Yourself in a Box, 311

Q

Questioning is OK, 104

R

Random Acts of Kindness, 204
Recognizing Our Oneness, 132
Recycling, 75
Relationships, Difficult, 291
Relationships, Love, 243
Release of Fear, 235
Respect for Each Other,
  Showing, 102
Respecting Diversity, 155
Respecting Someone Else's
  Property, 28
Responsibility, Growing in, 269
Reticence or Speaking
  Directly, 296
Reverence for Life, Showing, 195
Role Models, 38

S

School, Why Do I Need to
  Go to, 228
Secrets, Telling, 26
Secure, Feeling, 81
Seeking Balance, 212

Seeing the Bigger Picture, 314
Self Talk, Listen to, 159
Selfishness, Greed and, 238
Separated From God, When
  You Feel, 136
Serenity Prayer, 231
Setting Boundaries, 255
Setting Goals, 55
Sexual Harassment, 327
Shame, 211
Showing Appreciation, 44
Showing Respect for Each
  Other, 102
Showing Reverence for Life, 195
Shy, Being, 262
Singing Songs, 198
Singling Out Someone, 276
Smiles and Greetings, 187
Social Poise, 338
Socializing, 363
Sports, Playing, 141
Spring, There's Hope, 79
St. Patrick, Honoring, 76
St. Valentine's Day, 45
Stealing, 233
Stories, Telling, 199
Strategies, Win-Win, 151
Strengths and Weaknesses,
  Determining, 71
Stress, Handling, 119
Structure or No Structure?, 326
Struggles, 225
Study the Past to Ensure a
  Brighter Future, 321
Suicide, 140
Summer Solstice, 171
Summer Vacation, Preparing
  for, 135
Superstitions, 331

T

Take a Stroll, 324
Taking Time Out for My Self, 35

Team Player, Being a, 68
Teacher to Others, You Are a, 220
Teasing, 166
Telling Lies, 131
Telling Secrets, 26
Telling Stories, 199
Thanksgiving, 332
Think Healthy, 315
Thoughts, The Power of Your, 223
Tired of School, 46
Timing, 253
Traditions and Rituals, 261
Trashing the Earth, 196
Treasures of Heart and Mind, 264
Treatment of Family Members, 267
Trouble, Getting Someone Else in, 214
True Measure of a Person, The, 256
True Value of Our Things, 101
Trust, Building, 24
Trusting in Your Higher Power, 15
Trying to Move Too Quickly, 252
Trying New Things, 96
TV and Advertising, Monitoring, 106

U

Unconditional Love, 242
Unlimited Possibilities, 239
Unselfishness, 6
Unworthy or Fear of Success, Feeling, 107

V

Value of Money, 348
Value of Our Things, The True, 101
Violence, Eliminating, 109

Virtual Reality, 219
Vision, Having, 280

W

Walking into a Brick Wall, 221
Walls People Construct Between Themselves, Dealing With, 146
We Can Make Choices To Be Healthy, 124
What A Difference One Person Can Make, 29
What Am I Best at Doing, 73
What Do I Want To Be When I Grow Up! 77
When It's Spring, There Is Hope, 79
When Things Seem Overwhelming, 36
When You Feel Separated From God, 136
Whining and Complaining, 207
Who We Are, Finding Out, 50
Who Are Your Teachers? 218
Whose Problem Is It? 287
Why Am I Here? 123
Why Do I Need To Go To School, 228
Winners and Losers, 114
Winning Attitude A, 210
Winter Solstice, Time for Quiet Reflection, 355
Win-Win Strategies, 151
Worthiness, 72

Y

Year End Evaluation, Doing a, 366
You Are a Teacher to Others, 220
You Are Being Guided, 244
You Can't Please Everyone, 200

BIBLIOGRAPHY

Diane Keefe has participated on many boards serving teens and children. She has always been proactive in matters dealing with teens. She was recognized by the Ohio Senate for her service to the community while leading a teen center effort. In 1981/82 she was listed in *Who's Who in American Women* for her freelance writing for a technical association. She is a former home economics teacher who enjoys gardening, landscaping, decorating, and reading a good book. Currently, she resides in Missouri with her husband and two teenage daughters.

LIFELINES PUBLISHING ORDER FORM

Qty	Item	Single Price	Quantity Price
____	*Daily Lifelines for Teens & Preteens*	16.95	_____
____	*Seminar and Book Signing Schedule*	00	_____
	S & H	3.95	
	MO. Taxes ($.97 per book)	_____	_____
	Total Price	_____	_____

Payment type:

_____ Check   _____ Money Order

Credit: _____ VISA   _____ MasterCard

_____ Discover   _____ American Express

Card Number: _____   Exp. Date _____

Name on Card: _____

Signature: _____

Ship to:

Name: _____

Address: _____

City/State/Zip Code: _____

Date: _____   Phone (____) _____

Send check or money order to:
Book Masters, Inc.
P. O. Box 388
Ashland, OH 44805

Phone and credit card orders: 800-247-6553
email: order@Bookmaster.com

Visit our Website: www.LifelinesPublishing.com
Please allow 2-4 weeks delivery